"Voddie Baucham's book is both scri
ciples, cultural trends, and human nat
expository approach, by which he bri
conversation. I recommend it as an excellent introduction to apologetics as
it needs to be practiced today."

John M. Frame, J. D. Trimble Chair of Systematic Theology and
Philosophy, Reformed Theological Seminary, Orlando

"I am a fan of any book that takes apologetics out of the tower and puts
it in the pew. Baucham does a wonderful job of just that. His pastoral
style and sensitivity stand out as he takes a method of apologetics straight
from the Scriptures and lays out how everyone can defend the faith with
confidence."

C. Michael Patton, Founder, President, and fellow, The Credo House,
Edmond, Oklahoma

"Voddie Baucham's expository approach to apologetics reminds us of the
power of God's Word for responding to objections to the Christian faith.
This book hits all the right notes and guides the reader to think biblically,
confessionally, and theologically when engaging with those who reject
Christianity. Baucham's book will encourage the church to engage unbelief
from the perspective of Scripture, rather than from a lesser perspective."

K. Scott Oliphint, Professor of Apologetics and Systematic Theology,
Westminster Theological Seminary; author, *Covenantal Apologetics*

"Any biblical apologetic must rely on the Bible itself for its content and
its force. Exposing the Bible in clear and cogent theological categories is
essential for apologetics. By learning and applying the truths of this book,
Christians can become better prepared to give a defense of the hope that
is within them."

Douglas Groothuis, Professor of Philosophy and Director of
the Apologetics and Ethics Master's Degree, Denver Seminary;
author, *Christian Apologetics*

Expository Apologetics

Other Crossway Books by Voddie Baucham

Joseph and the Gospel of Many Colors: Reading an Old Story in a New Way (2013)

Family Shepherds: Calling and Equipping Men to Lead Their Homes (2011)

What He Must Be: . . . If He Wants to Marry My Daughter (2009)

Family Driven Faith: Doing What It Takes to Raise Sons and Daughters Who Walk with God (2007)

EXPOSITORY APOLOGETICS

Answering Objections
with the
Power of the Word

VODDIE BAUCHAM JR.

CROSSWAY®

WHEATON, ILLINOIS

Expository Apologetics: Answering Objections with the Power of the Word

Copyright © 2015 by Voddie Baucham Jr.

Published by Crossway
        1300 Crescent Street
        Wheaton, Illinois 60187

Published in association with Yates & Yates, www.yates2.com

Cover design: Jeff Miller, Faceout Studio

First printing 2015

Printed in the United States of America

Trade paperback ISBN: 978-1-4335-3379-2
ePub ISBN: 978-1-4335-3382-2
PDF ISBN: 978-1-4335-3380-8
Mobipocket ISBN: 978-1-4335-3381-5

Library of Congress Cataloging-in-Publication Data
Baucham, Voddie.
   Expository apologetics : answering objections with the power of the word / Voddie Baucham, Jr.
     pages cm.
   Includes bibliographical references and index.
   ISBN 978-1-4335-3379-2 (tp)
   1. Apologetics. 2. Preaching. I. Title.
BT1103.B38   2015
239—dc23   2014045702

Crossway is a publishing ministry of Good News Publishers.

VP   31   30   29   28   27   26   25   24   23   22
20   19   18   17   16   15   14   13   12   11   10

To David Shiflet
My friend, brother, and colaborer
for the sake of the gospel
and the man who encouraged me
to write this book

Contents

Acknowledgments

This book was born out of a conversation with my dear friend and colaborer, David Shiflet. I am grateful for his insightful and inquisitive mind that led him to see something in my preaching and teaching that I had not seen. I am also grateful for his willingness to engage me in conversations that led to greater clarity and insight on both his part and mine. Finally, I am grateful for his insistence that I write a book about what he helped me to clarify and systematize.

Special thanks are also due to those who make it possible for me to devote what little time I have to writing books. I am thankful to God for my wife, Bridget, for her support, encouragement, and steadfast love. I am grateful to my children for their contributions to my work. To Jasmine for her help in research, to Trey for our discussions, to Elijah, Asher, Judah, Micah, and Safya for their participation and engagement in catechism and family worship that have helped me put the pieces together. And to Amos and Simeon who, though too young to be engaged fully in the process right now (ages two and one at the time of this writing), the fact that God has given you to me serves as motivation to carry on in this great adventure of parenting and disciple making.

Finally, I am grateful to God for the people of Grace Family Baptist Church and my fellow elders who have labored alongside me during the development and writing of this material. To Joshua Loyd and Dale Ashworth, with whom I labored during the development of this project, and Stephen Bratton, who has been with me from the beginning to the end, I owe a debt of gratitude that can neither be expressed adequately nor repaid. I thank God for their partnership in the gospel and their support of my writing ministry.

Introduction

Several years ago, a dear friend and brother came to me with a proposal that would change the trajectory of my ministry. We were working together in a leadership/elder training program in our local church. I was teaching a section on preaching, and he asked me a simple question, "Have you ever thought about formalizing the process you use to do that thing you do in your preaching?" He was curious as to whether (1) I was doing it on purpose, (2) I had a process I used to do it, and (3) it was something that could be taught to others.

Of course, that question led to a number of discussions about "that thing I do." They centered around a tendency I had to argue with myself during sermons. I would make a point, then immediately say something like, "I know what you're thinking . . ." I would then express common objections to the proposition I had just made, then proceed to answer those objections.

People would come up to me and say things like, "That was exactly what I was thinking," or, "I had a discussion with someone the other day and that is *exactly* what he said." People referred to this as "relevance" or "insightfulness" in my messages and interactions. However, David Shiflet saw something else. He saw a consistent application of a set of techniques that shaped the way I dealt with certain issues. Eventually, I gave that *thing* a name. I called it *expository apologetics. Expository* because it was based in my commitment to expository preaching. *Apologetics* because it was essentially about answering objections.

Of course, as I explored, I discovered that this process did not originate with me. The more I listened and evaluated what was going on, the more familiar it sounded. When our pulpit ministry turned its attention to preaching through Romans, I found the source of my method. I was doing nothing more than imitating Paul's common practice in Romans. I had gravitated to it because of my own background and experience, and it had become second nature. However, what I was doing in my sermons was definitely not new.

Having grown up in a non-Christian home and come to the gospel late, I am accustomed to looking at Scripture through the lens of a skeptic. While I am grateful that my children are growing up surrounded by and saturated with the gospel, I see the unique perspective God gave me as a result of my experience, and am grateful that he has used it to shape my understanding and approach. Had I not been an "outsider," I probably would have looked at Paul's use of the questions of his interlocutors and moved on. However, having walked in the shoes of those who asked those pointed questions, I could not shake Paul's approach. I was drawn to it. I imbibed it!

This book is an attempt to introduce a new way of thinking about apologetics, which is actually not new at all. At its core, it is a practical expression of presuppositional apologetics. However, instead of discussing the various approaches to apologetics, or the broader issues associated most commonly with apologetics, this book is about the *nature* and *practice* of apologetics.

The goal here is not to advance a new set of arguments for the existence of God, or to tackle the question of evil and suffering, or to debate origins. The goal here is to introduce an approach to apologetics that is accessible and effective. The audience is everyone who claims faith in Christ through the power of the gospel.

Despite popular opinion, apologetics is not a discipline for elite Christians. Nor is the practice of apologetics limited to formal debate. Apologetics is as practical as anything in the Christian life. Every believer is required and expected to be an apologist (1 Pet. 3:15). As such, every believer is required and expected to think and prepare like an apologist. Of course, if apologetics is the highly philosophical, formal process we have come to expect, this sounds like an impossible task for most Christians. However, if apologetics is as simple as knowing what we believe and why we believe it, and being able to communicate that to others in a humble, winsome, biblical manner, that's a horse of a different color!

It is this latter definition to which this book is devoted. Thank God for apologists who can stand up at Harvard, Stanford, or Oxford and debate leading scientists on the origin of man and the Genesis account. It is a blessing to have men like James White who can stand toe-to-toe with leading Islamic scholars and debate the intricate nuances of the New Testament with references to the original languages, textual variants, and manuscript counts, all while referring to the Qur'an in the original Arabic and distinguishing between auras written in Mecca and those written in Medina. However, the majority of Christians will never have the capacity or the opportunity to do any of this. And if our definition of apologetics does not encompass more than this, most Christians will think it's not for them, it's for the "experts."

But once we understand apologetics to be an essential part of the Christian life and experience, and see those formal debaters as no more than Christians who are using their particular training to apply the basic principles to a different context, then we can see ourselves rightly and engage at whatever level we are able. That is the heart of expository apologetics! Not only *can* you be an apologist; you *must* be! Once you understand that, your understanding and approach change. Then comes the question, "Where do I start?" That's where this book comes in.

We begin by defining apologetics and placing it in its biblical and theological context. This includes a discussion of Peter's foundational teaching in 1 Peter 3 and Paul's teaching in Romans. The focus then shifts to the practical application of apologetics, including the importance of creeds, catechisms, and confessions as tools for preparation, the interactive "expository apologetics waltz" as a model for individual interaction, and the application of expository apologetics to preaching, teaching, and disciple making. We conclude with an example of an expository apologetic sermon.

What Is Expository
Apologetics?

In the fall of 1987, I met a man whom God would use to change my life. Steve Morgan was a Campus Crusade staffer. It was my first year of college, and my first year as a starter on the football team. Not many true freshmen play, let alone start in their first game in Division 1 college football. This was a big deal. It was such a big deal that everyone knew my name, including Steve Morgan. However, while the rest of the campus was abuzz because of my prowess on the field, Steve had other ideas.

Steve had heard that I was a Christian. This was welcome news to a young man committed to spreading the gospel on a college campus. One day he simply walked into the locker room and introduced himself. I reciprocated, and a relationship that would span decades was born. However, Steve had been misinformed. I wasn't a Christian. In fact, I didn't know much at all about Christianity. So his encounter with me was not at all what Steve expected.

I was raised in South Central Los Angeles at a time when drugs, gangs, and violence were common fare. My mother was a single parent. She gave birth to me shortly after her eighteenth birthday. She and my father married, because that's what you did in 1969. However, their marriage lasted only a couple of years. From then on it was just the two us. And no, my mother didn't raise me in church. She was a Buddhist.

Steve figured out very quickly that he wasn't talking to a fellow believer. And like the soul-winner he was and is, immediately he turned the conversation to the gospel. But he figured out that his "four spiritual laws" approach was not going to be effective with someone with my spiritual background. So the Wisconsin native and Green Bay Packers fan did his best Vince Lombardi imitation. Steve held up his Bible and, mimicking Vince's famous "Men, this is a football" line, said, "Voddie, *this* is a Bible." From that day on we spent weeks examining the claims of Christ.

In this process, I would ask questions, and Steve would answer them. If he didn't have an answer, he got back to me. About two weeks into this process, however, he began to show me how to find the answers myself. I have often said that I was trained in apologetics before I was even converted. But converted I was! Friday, November 13, 1987. Steve was coming to meet me, but he was late. While I sat waiting, I realized I didn't have any more questions. I also realized that God was at work in my heart. I lay down on the floor in the locker room, and, in my own simplistic way, I repented of my sin and placed my faith in Christ. Steve came in and we rejoiced together.

However, I also mourned that day. As we sat there together, I wept. All I could think about was a cousin with whom I had grown up in Los Angeles. Jarmal was like the brother I never had. Steve slapped me on the back and said, "Let's go call him." I looked at him through tear-stained eyes and replied, "I can't. He was killed in a drug deal in Oakland last year. I watched him being lowered into the ground about six months before the start of my freshman year."

Steve did two things that day that I will always appreciate and never forget. First, he did not try to come up with a mystical explanation that would assuage my pain by assuring me of Jarmal's place in heaven. Second, he turned my focus from the pain of my sudden realization to the hope I had yet to realize. He said, very simply, "What about other people you need to call?" I then reached out to everyone I knew and told them about my new-found faith. I simply started with the Bible and the claims of Christ. I gave answers where I could, and when I didn't have answers, I searched until I found them.

Thus was born my passion for souls and my penchant for apologetics. From that day to this, I remain grateful to Steve Morgan and committed to doing for others what he did for me: introducing them to Jesus Christ through bearing with them patiently and passionately, believing that the Lord will use the gospel to save his people (Rom. 1:16). Make no mistake: I am committed to apologetics as a consequence of my commitment to evangelism. This is not about winning arguments; it's about winning souls. My desire is that Christ might have the fullness of the reward for which he died.

If legitimate objections are standing between someone and his embrace of Christ, I want to address those objections and point him to Christ. In fact, when I encounter such objections, I assume that God has placed me in that conversation by his providence in order to give an answer for the hope that is in me (1 Pet. 3:15). I do not see my presence in a person's life as a tool of condemnation, "for God did not send his Son into the world to condemn the world, but in order that the world might be saved through him" (John 3:17).

Nor is this understanding contradicted by my belief in predestination. As Loraine Boettner contends:

> The objection that the doctrine of Predestination discourages all motives to exertion, is based on the fallacy that the ends are determined without reference to the means. It is not merely a few isolated events here and there that have been foreordained, but the whole chain of events, with all of their inter-relations and connections. All of parts form a unit in the Divine plan. If the means should fail, so would the ends. If God has purposed that a man shall reap, He has also purposed that he shall sow. If God has ordained a man to be saved, He has also ordained that he shall hear the Gospel, and that he shall believe and repent. As well might the farmer refuse to till the soil according to the laws disclosed by the light of nature and experience until he had first learned what was the secret purpose of God to be executed in His providence in regard to the fruitfulness of the coming season, as for any one to refuse to work in the moral and spiritual realms because he does not know what fruitage God may bring from his labor. We find, however, that the fruitage is commonly bestowed where the preliminary work has been faithfully performed. If we engage in the Lord's service and make diligent use of the means which He has prescribed, we have the great

encouragement of knowing that it is by these very means that He has determined to accomplish His great work.[1]

The use of means, then, is completely consistent with the belief in sovereign predestination. Let no one embrace the lie of hyper-Calvinism and neglect his duty to preach the gospel: "For if I preach the gospel, that gives me no ground for boasting. For necessity is laid upon me. Woe to me if I do not preach the gospel!" (1 Cor. 9:16). To that end, let us examine apologetics from the understanding that it is to aid gospel proclamation.

DEFINING EXPOSITORY APOLOGETICS

In its simplest form, apologetics is knowing what we believe and why we believe it, and being able to communicate that to others effectively (Titus 1:9; 1 Pet. 3:15; Jude 1–4). Expository apologetics is merely the application of the principles of biblical exposition to the art and science of apologetics. It is based on the inerrancy, infallibility, sufficiency, and authority of the Bible. This approach to apologetics is not based on acquiring the latest knowledge in fields like astronomy, geology, physics, psychology, or comparative religion. This approach is based on the believer's need to have a firm grasp on basic truths and a willingness to share those truths when and where opportunities arise. Our view is always toward gospel proclamation.

In its simplest form, expository apologetics is about three things. First, it is about being biblical. We answer objections with the power of the Word. Second, it is about being easy to remember. If we can't remember this simplicity, we won't use it in our everyday encounters. Third, it is about being conversational. We must be able to share truth in a manner that is natural, reasonable, and winsome.

I'm not talking about preparing to defeat Christopher Hitchens in a formal debate. The goal here is to be able to answer him or anyone else in the normal flow of everyday conversation as you share your faith in a natural way. This is about freeing you up to do what every believer is called, commanded, and expected to do in the process of living out the Christian life. There are "things most surely believed among us" (Luke 1:1), and we ought to be prepared to defend them.

The picture of apologetics as formal debate is what often keeps "normal" Christians from pursuing the subject. We think, "That kind of debate is not consistent with my personality, nor with my gifting/ training, therefore, I must not be called to apologetics." Consequently, we not only take a pass on apologetics; we feel completely justified in doing so. All the while, a biblical mandate is staring us in the face.

Expository apologetics takes into account the fact that the gospel, by its very nature, is limited and limiting. It is limited because we are operating from a closed canon. No new truths are being revealed. It is limiting because the objections that must be answered cannot exceed the propositions being put forth. Thus, there are a limited number of objections. Additionally, the objections to the gospel are not new. In fact, there was much more opposition to the gospel in the early days of the church, when the truths being proclaimed were new and radical, than there are now after two millennia have passed and those objections have been asked and answered again and again.

If there are a limited number of objections to the gospel message, and these objections have been answered by biblical authors under the inspiration of the Holy Spirit, then their answers will certainly be more effective and authoritative than any we could devise on our own (Prov. 30:5; 2 Tim. 3:16,17; 2 Pet. 1:20–21). Moreover, it is incumbent upon us to present these arguments in a clear, concise manner while paying close attention to the historical, grammatical, and contextual issues surrounding the biblical texts (2 Tim. 2:15). This, in essence, is expository apologetics.

DEFINING APOLOGETICS

Cornelius Van Til defined apologetics as "the vindication of the Christian philosophy of life against the various forms of the non-Christian philosophy of life."[2] This will serve as the philosophical baseline for our approach to expository apologetics. When we preach or teach, when we witness to a stranger, or when we are making disciples in our home or church, it is important to keep this definition in mind. We stand before people who have been bombarded every day of their lives by philosophies of life that contradict Christianity. When they open their Bibles, they are rarely aware of how many presuppositions they bring to the encounter, let alone how contradictory they are. They need someone willing to vindicate a Christian philosophy of life.

This is not the same as vindicating ourselves, or our own opinions (Rom. 12:19–21). The object of this vindication is God's truth. Nor is our approach to this vindication left to chance. An examination of the principal apologetics texts in the New Testament reveals at least three forms this vindication should take. We will take them in order of magnitude from the least confrontational to the most.

Vindication through Answering Objections

The least confrontational/aggressive form of vindication is answering objections. People may have objections to the Christian faith for a variety of reasons. Some have never heard the message. Others have never understood it. Still others have had experiences that seem to contradict it. Regardless of why these objections exist, the fact is, they present us with an opportunity to provide an answer. This is the message of 1 Peter: "But in your hearts honor Christ the Lord as holy, always being prepared to make a defense to anyone who asks you for a reason for the hope that is in you; yet do it with gentleness and respect" (1 Pet. 3:15).

I'll say much more about this in chapter 9. For now, it is enough to note that we have clear biblical evidence and examples of this first kind of vindication of the Christian faith. All believers are called to engage in this practice.

Vindication through Wrestling with Error

The second way we are called upon to vindicate the Christian philosophy of life against the various forms of the non-Christian philosophy of life is by wrestling with error.

> Jude, a servant of Jesus Christ and brother of James, To those who are called, beloved in God the Father and kept for Jesus Christ: May mercy, peace, and love be multiplied to you. Beloved, although I was very eager to write to you about our common salvation, I found it necessary to write appealing to you to contend for the faith that was once for all delivered to the saints. For certain people have crept in unnoticed who long ago were designated for this condemnation,

ungodly people, who pervert the grace of our God into sensuality and deny our only Master and Lord, Jesus Christ." (Jude 1–4)

This wrestling can take many forms.

First, we must wrestle with our own contradictions and inconsistencies. We are frail, fragile, sinful people. And we live in a fallen, evil world that opposes our God, his Christ, and his gospel. Thus, between our own fallenness and the falseness of the world around us, there are innumerable areas where our thinking is compromised. It is naive to think that we have it all figured out. Therefore, we "destroy arguments and every lofty opinion raised against the knowledge of God, and take every thought captive to obey Christ, being ready to punish every disobedience, when your obedience is complete" (2 Cor. 10:5–6). We do this, at least in part, through refusing to be "conformed to this world, but [by being] transformed by the renewal of your mind, that by testing you may discern what is the will of God, what is good and acceptable and perfect" (Rom. 12:2).

Second, we must wrestle with contradictions that come to us directly. Have you ever met one of those heresy hunters? You know, those people who ask you theological questions not because they desire to learn or to engage in thoughtful Christian dialogue, but because they're checking to see where your "flaws" are? Unfortunately, I have run into far too many people like that.

I remember a pastor's conference I spoke at a few years back. I remember it so well because I was as sick as a dog. It was one of those trips where I arrived at the hotel, asked for some medicine, then told the host not to bother calling me for dinner. The next day, things were no better. Nevertheless, I preached my guts out. I love preaching, but I love preaching to preachers most. It is both a blessing and an honor. And this time in particular, God was extremely kind to me. Pastors were approaching me to tell me how encouraged they were, and to compliment my keen insights and applications. Then it happened!

I was lying under a table waiting to preach the final time. That's right: I was so sick I couldn't stand and sing. I found a book table in the back of the room that I could lie under and asked someone to alert me just before it was time for me to preach. Just then a thoughtful pastor came by and asked if he could pray for me. "Absolutely!" I said as I closed my eyes and came up to my knees. When he finished praying, he leaned over and said, "I don't think I've ever heard finer preaching, or seen better handling of the Word. I just can't believe you would use a modern translation and not the 'authorized version.'" This type of "heresy hunting" is a perfect example of the kinds of contradictions with which we must be prepared to wrestle.

Third, we must wrestle with the contradictions that we know to be common among those whom we are responsible to teach. This is as true for the parent as it is for the pastor. Whenever God places us in a teaching position, part of our responsibility is to root out contradictions in the lives of our hearers. If I am aware of ideas contrary to the truth of God's Word that are plaguing and corrupting the thinking of those who sit under my teaching, it is only natural for me to address it, and to do so in a normal, natural, scriptural way.

Paul writes of the elder: "He must hold firm to the trustworthy word as taught, so that he may be able to give instruction in sound doctrine and also to rebuke those who contradict it" (Titus 1:9).

THE NEED FOR APOLOGETICS

Apologetics has waxed and waned in terms of its popularity among Christians in America. At times there has been more emphasis on mercy ministry, social outreach, or church growth. At other times evangelism and apologetics take center stage. Currently, we are in the midst of a surge in the popularity and practice of apologetics. More and more, Christians are beginning to recognize the need. Apologetics is necessary today because of issues such as biblical illiteracy, postmodern/post-Christian thinking, open opposition to biblical truth, and the growing presence of opposing religions.

Biblical Illiteracy

One foundational reason why we need apologetics is the basic biblical illiteracy we find in both the culture at large and in the church. People simply do not know what the Bible says. People don't read the Bible anymore. As a result, some of the most basic tenets of Christianity, ones that once would have been known and assumed to be true by most Americans, are today considered obscure and suspect.

Almost no one knows the Ten Commandments anymore, let alone believes that they are relevant. And catechesis is a foreign concept even to the most committed Christians. As a result, our culture is no longer filled with people who grew up steeped in these basic ideas. Today, not even those who attended church as children have heard foundational biblical truths. Consequently, we cannot assume anything. We must be prepared to defend the most basic claims and ideas of our faith.

Postmodern/Post-Christian Thinking

The belief that truth is relative directly opposes the concept of apologetics. I learned this the hard way when I was a student at Oxford. I was finishing one doctoral program in the United States while simultaneously starting another doctoral program in the United Kingdom. My first week at Oxford, I was introduced to my primary instructor, Dr. M. When he learned that I was an American working on an apologetics-oriented dissertation back in the United States, he immediately set out to chart a course for me that included reading and writing on the subjects of inclusivism and pluralism. It was a very trying time.

I came face-to-face with postmodernism in its most powerful form. Here I was in the third oldest and arguably most respected university on planet Earth, and everywhere I turned truth was being denied, ambiguity affirmed, and certainty vilified. I had to learn very quickly how to hold my own and defend my faith among academic elites. I also learned that academic elites were just making slightly more sophisticated attempts at the same arguments with which I was familiar. In the end, I used the power of the Word to shape my arguments and forced others to acknowledge their lack of authoritative support.

Open Opposition to Biblical Truth

Another issue giving rise to the resurgence of apologetics is the open opposition to biblical truth prevalent in Western society. Gone are the days when the truths of the Bible were assumed and men held accountable to them. Today, Christianity is seen as a threat to freedom, or even a pathological condition. Schools accept the "theory" of evolution, but view the idea of creation as a dangerous myth. Judges see the biblical view of sodomy as a hate crime. In fact, Child Protective Services has at times listed regular church attendance as one of the hallmarks of abusive parenting.[3]

In this landscape, Christians must have a ready answer for those who believe that we are not just wrong—we are evil. Expository apologetics can be a powerful tool in the midst of such opposition. I am not proposing that the ideas outlined in this book will necessarily shut the mouths of our detractors. That is the job of the Holy Spirit. However, we can most certainly expose their hypocrisy and point them to the truth using the powerful, active, two-edged sword at our disposal.

Opposing Religions

The contemporary idea of religious freedom is a modern invention. People today believe that the Pilgrims had Muslims, Buddhists, and Hindus in mind when they crossed the ocean to be free to worship God. However, a cursory glance at history dispels that myth. For example, both the Mayflower Compact and the Charter of New England make it very clear that the freedom early American settlers sought was not the freedom of syncretism or pluralism, but the freedom to advance the gospel of Jesus Christ:

> We according to our princely Inclination, favouring much their worthy Disposition, in Hope thereby to advance the in Largement of Christian Religion, to the Glory of God Almighty . . . [4]

These days are long gone. Today Christian exclusivity is numbered among the greatest evils in the land. It's wicked and un-American! How ironic.

THREE AUDIENCES OF EXPOSITORY APOLOGETICS

So who is this book for? Which Christians need to be concerned about expository apologetics? This is a question that drives me crazy! When I entered the publishing world, I learned very quickly that "you can't write for everybody . . . you have to pick an audience." Well, this book literally *is* for everybody. Why? Because apologetics is for everybody.

Because apologetics is for everybody, this book is for everyone. But I realize that I cannot write specific applications for every Christian in every conceivable situation. As such, I have had to narrow my focus a bit. I have done so by identifying three main audiences with whom readers of this book might interact.

The first audience is the heathen. This is the person who is both ignorant of and antagonistic toward the gospel. This audience requires an evangelist. The second audience is the churchgoer. This is a person who, whether converted or unconverted, is sitting under the regular preaching and teaching of the Word. This audience requires a preacher/ teacher. The final audience is the disciple. This person is brand new to the things of God. This is the child being raised in the discipline and instruction of the Lord (Eph. 6:4), or the new convert unlearning and relearning everything he thinks he knows.

The Evangelist as Expository Apologist

The evangelist is the most obvious audience of this book. He is confident, energetic, engaging, and active in bringing the gospel to bear in conversations with non-Christians. For the evangelist, expository apologetics is an invaluable tool. He must be equipped and prepared to confront ideas that stand opposed to the Christian world and life view.

Much of this book is targeted toward the evangelist. That is because whether we are evangelists, preachers/teachers, or disciples, our goal is the same. As expository apologists, we point people to Christ and call them to repent and believe. We are constantly showing people how foolish and dangerous it is to trust in anything but Christ. At bottom, the expository apologist is an evangelist.

However, here we are talking about evangelism in the truest, most comprehensive sense of the word. The kind of evangelism envisioned in the Great Commission:

> All authority in heaven and on earth has been given to me. Go therefore and make disciples of all nations, baptizing them in the name of the Father and of the Son and of the Holy Spirit, teaching them to observe all that I have commanded you. And behold, I am with you always, to the end of the age. (Matt. 28:18–20)

Evangelism is more than merely convincing people of the rightness of Christianity or getting them to walk an aisle and pray a prayer. Evangelism is about making disciples—calling people away from the kingdom of man and into the kingdom of God. This kind of transfer of allegiance is at the heart of expository apologetics.

For the evangelist, the most important aspects of expository apologetics are (1) why unbelief exists (see chap. 3) and (2) knowing how to turn any conversation into an expository apologetic opportunity (see chap. 7). Ironically, while the evangelist is the most obvious candidate for expository apologetics, he is not the candidate most likely to use it on the most consistent basis.

The Preacher/Teacher as Expository Apologist

While the evangelist is the most obvious audience of this book, the preacher/teacher is the reason I wrote it. For years people have commented on the uniqueness of my preaching. Most people simply offer kind words of thanks. Others, however, have put their finger on what it is they see as distinct. One man put it best when he said, "It is as though you see the text as an outsider."

What he was trying to say is that I have a tendency not to assume things where others most likely would. I often argue with myself during a sermon, taking on the persona of someone who disagrees with what I'm saying and then answering the objection. I think psychologists have a name for that, and psychiatrists have a drug for it. However, I have managed to avoid treatment long enough to figure out what I've been doing all these years and to give it the name *expository apologetics*.

What follows here is an attempt to help other teachers do the same. I want to encourage them to look at a text and ask, "What questions does this text raise?" or "What doctrine am I expounding, and what objections are common?" and, "What would a person hostile to the gospel be thinking if they heard me say this?" These are just a few of the questions that can turn any sermon or lesson into an exercise in expository apologetics.

Nor is this to say that everything we do should be geared toward the unbeliever. In fact, I am not talking about the unbeliever at all here. Unlike the evangelist, the pastor/teacher is, for the most part, dealing with

Christians. However, Christians have areas of unbelief and doubt. They live in a world that is constantly challenging their thinking both overtly and covertly. They watch television, go to school, read magazines and newspapers, surf the Internet, and interact daily with people and things that influence their thinking. They need to be reminded constantly of the apostle's admonition: "Do not be conformed to this world, but be transformed by the renewing of your mind" (Rom. 12:1).

Doing this requires constant vigilance. The pastor/teacher must always be ready and able to "give instruction in sound doctrine and also to rebuke those who contradict it" (Titus 1:9). He must be on guard, "for the time is coming when people will not endure sound teaching, but having itching ears they will accumulate for themselves teachers to suit their own passions, and will turn away from listening to the truth and wander off into myths" (2 Tim. 4:3–4). Expository apologetics is a bulwark against the tendency to forget how hard it is to believe in the face of constant opposition.

For the pastor/teacher, the most important elements of expository apologetics are (1) finding and teaching expository apologetic texts and (2) turning any text into an expository apologetic opportunity.

The Discipler as Expository Apologist

Interestingly, the one least likely to be considered an apologist is the one most likely to engage in expository apologetics. Neither the evangelist nor the pastor/teacher will have a fraction of the expository apologetic encounters the discipler will. The discipler is a parent raising children or the more mature believer taking a new believer by the hand and introducing him or her to the fundamental truths of the Christian faith.

Think about it: apologetics is about knowing what we believe and why we believe it, and being able to communicate that to others in a clear, cogent, winsome manner. It's all about answering questions posed by skeptics. What are our children? Some of them are people who do not believe. They are ignorant. They are curious. They ask questions. Lots and lots of questions, all the time. And we need to be ready and able to answer those questions. Hence, expository apologetics!

As parents we have a tremendous opportunity to shape the faith of our children. We can either do that well or we can do it poorly, but we will do it. View this book as a guide to help you map out a right way— not *the* right way, but at least *a* right way. For the discipler, expository apologetics is a means of following the apostle's admonition: "Fathers, do not provoke your children to anger, but bring them up in the discipline and instruction of the Lord" (Eph. 6:4).

There are millions of Christian parents who have gone before you, and they have provided paths on which to tread. They used mysterious tools called catechism, formative discipline, Christian education, and family worship. I have written about all of these. However, I have yet to spend a great deal of time on catechism. I intend to change that here. I believe catechism is the best apologetics training tool we have at our disposal. Please note that I did not say "the best training tool *for children*." I believe it's the best tool, period.

This incredible duty to prepare the next generation to hold and defend the truth we confess has long been the goal of Christian parents. In fact, in the preface to the Second London Baptist Confession, the authors make this point quite clear:

> And verily there is one spring and cause of the decay of Religion in our day, which we cannot but touch upon, and earnestly urge a redresse of; and that is the neglect of the worship of God in Families, by those to whom the charge and conduct of them is committed. May not the grosse ignorance, and instability of many; with the prophaneness of others, be justly charged upon their Parents and Masters; who have not trained them up in the way wherein they ought to walk when they were young? but have neglected those frequent and solemn commands which the Lord hath laid upon them so to catechize, and instruct them, that their tender years might be seasoned with the knowledge of the truth of God as revealed in the Scriptures; and also by their own omission of Prayer, and other duties of Religion in their families, together with the ill example of their loose conversation, have inured them first to a neglect, and then contempt of all Piety and Religion? We know this will not excuse the blindness, or wickedness of any; but certainly it will fall heavy upon those that have thus been the occasion thereof; they indeed dye in their sins; but will not their blood be required of those under whose care they were, who yet permitted them to go on

without warning, yea led them into the paths of destruction? And will not the diligence of Christians with respect to the discharge of these duties, in ages past, rise up in judgment against, and condemn many of those who would be esteemed such now?

Our responsibility as parents is to teach our children those things most surely believed among us. And as we do that, we must do it with a view toward equipping them to always be "prepared to make a defense to anyone who asks [them] for a reason for the hope that is in [them]" (1 Pet. 3:15). This is the goal of expository apologetics.

But what about disciplers who are working with people who are not their children? What about the person working with new converts or those who are not quite converted? The answer is simple: treat them like children! In other words, adult new believers also need their questions answered. And they need systematic roadmaps laid out before them. This is the same thing we do as we disciple our children. Thus, expository apologetics has much to offer the nonparent discipler.

For the discipler, the most important elements of expository apologetics are (1) the role of the law in expository apologetics (chap. 7) and (2) using catechism as an expository apologetics training tool (chap. 5).

1 Peter 3 and the Essence of Apologetics

The 2014 Super Bowl was a study in contrasts. The Denver Broncos, a high-flying, offensive juggernaut, took on the ground-and-pound Seattle Seahawks in what was one of the most lopsided contests in the game's history—but not in the way people expected. Denver came in as the most high-scoring offense in NFL history. As the first team ever to score more than six hundred points in a single season, the Broncos, led by Peyton Manning, one of the best quarterbacks ever to play the game, were expected to handle the Seahawks and their second-year quarterback with relative ease. However, the game didn't turn out that way at all.

As we used to say, the Seahawks beat the snot out of the Broncos. It was a massacre. It was one of those games that went from entertaining to humiliating. By the second half it was hard to watch. But how did it happen? How was the most prolific offense in the history of the game reduced to rubble? How was the league's most valuable player left looking dazed, disoriented, and defeated? The answer is actually quite simple: Seattle executed the fundamentals of the game better than Denver did. They blocked better, they tackled better, they ran the ball better, they protected the ball better. They played knock-down-drag-out, smash-mouth football, and simply beat Denver up. They were more physical, more violent, and more passionate, and the result was complete domination.

I view expository apologetics in much the same way Seattle approached the 2014 Super Bowl. Apologetics is not about being cute or fancy; it's not about coming up with some new philosophical slight-of-hand or some argument people have never heard of. Expository apologetics is about doing the basics and doing them well. It's about playing with passion and confidence. It's about being consistent and methodical regardless of the odds or opposition.

What, then, are our basics? What constitutes our blocking, tackling, clock management, and sound defense? The answer to that question must be found in the Bible. And what better passage to begin than the very passage from which we get the word *apologetics*: 1 Peter 3?

My goal in this chapter is to look at this familiar passage in a way that makes it clear that Peter did not have a band of trained philosophers and intellectual giants in mind when he wrote, but rather all believers in the Lord Jesus Christ. Nor was he introducing a sophisticated approach to debate. He was simply telling Christians how to live and believe in light of the curiosity and opposition their faith would certainly encounter.

Also, we must understand the context of Peter's words since it sets the tone for our entire approach to expository apologetics. When we understand his words in their broader context, it becomes even clearer that Peter is speaking to Joe Christian, and not some high-minded professor. He is also speaking to weak, downtrodden, persecuted saints who needed to know how to give an answer in the midst of their adversity. This, too, is a far cry from the mental picture we are prone to paint when we think about apologetics.

THE APOSTLE PETER AND THE FOUNDATION OF APOLOGETICS

Anyone with the slightest interest in apologetics knows 1 Peter 3:15. After all, it is the very text from which we get our word *apologetics*. However, fewer people are familiar with the context of that verse, both the immediate paragraph to which it belongs and the section as a whole. As a result, some of the nuance is lost on us. And I am convinced that this is the cause of much confusion and fear concerning apologetics.

We view apologetics as primarily a philosophical endeavor to be employed only by those with quick, keen, nimble minds and specialized training. We also believe you have to be a bit of a jerk to be any good at it, since the primary goal, as we understand it, is to vanquish our foe and stand triumphantly atop his lifeless intellect with face lifted toward the heavens and chest swollen with pride. As a result, the average Christian not only believes he or she is intellectually inadequate to engage in apologetics but also has an aversion to the attitude associated with the practice.

This is both unfortunate and ironic. Unfortunate, because many Christians are actually disobeying God's Word by refusing to engage in apologetics. Ironic, because many Christians who are engaging in apologetics are actually doing it in a way that is inconsistent with the biblical mandate, and as a direct result are actually discouraging their brothers and sisters in the Lord. What's worse is the fact that these same Christians are raising and discipling their children in an anti-apologetic atmosphere that is actually detrimental to their understanding of the gospel and the Christian life.

I am convinced that when we understand Peter's teaching on apologetics we will see that (1) his admonition is for every Christian, (2) it has nothing to do with creating an elite, special forces brand of Christian, (3) it is rooted in the context of humility, holiness, and suffering, and (4) it ought to be a natural part of our Christian walk. Moreover, we will be far more likely to engage in this life-giving practice. And it all begins with discovering a lost paragraph.

THE LOST PARAGRAPH

Before we get to the immediate context of 1 Peter 3:15 (vv. 13–17), we must examine the broader context of Peter's admonition. In doing so, we will notice that there is a missing paragraph of sorts. What I am referring to is 1 Peter 3:8–12. We know the paragraph that follows it (at least in part) because of its teaching on apologetics. We also know the paragraph before it (vv. 1–7), since it is one of the Bible's famous "household code" passages (see also Eph. 5:22–33; Col. 3:18–22; Titus 2:5–10).[1] However, we are almost completely unfamiliar with the paragraph between these two familiar passages, or the broader context to which it belongs.

Nor is this mere exegetical novelty. It is this broader context that sheds light on Peter's teaching concerning apologetics and the attitude that should accompany it. Thus, it is impossible to understand the classic apologetic passage without first understanding the "lost paragraph" that precedes it: 3:8–12.

This lost paragraph belongs to a broader section of Peter's epistle which spans from 2:11 to 3:12. Hence, this paragraph is actually the conclusion of the section. The overarching message of this section is winning the respect of outsiders by your conduct. The section begins with the identification of the people of God as "sojourners and exiles" in the world (2:11–12). The apostle then proceeds to address three means through which the conduct of believers wins the respect of outsiders. All three involve humble, faithful submission to authority.

The occasion for such an admonition is clear from the historical context. As Calvin notes:

> By refusing the yoke of government, [Jewish Christians] would have given to the Gentiles no small occasion for reproaching them. And, indeed, the Jews were especially hated and counted infamous for this reason, because they were regarded on account of their perverseness as ungovernable. And as the commotions which they raised up in the provinces, were causes of great calamities, so that every one of a quiet and peaceable disposition dreaded them as the plague,—this was the reason that induced Peter to speak so strongly on subjection.[2]

In other words, this command was a matter of calling believers to live out their faith in ways that testified to the validity and impact of the gospel they preached and believed. Subjecting to authority is an act of obedience to God. Second, it is a witness to a watching world. Peter's instructions are similar to Paul's admonition in Titus to fulfill the household codes "that the word of God may not be reviled" (2:5), "so that an opponent may be put to shame, having nothing evil to say about us" (2:8), and "so that in everything [we] may adorn the doctrine of God our Savior" (2:10). Both audiences will be important to remember when we approach the apologetic text in 3:15.

In chapter 2 of his first epistle, Peter urges believers to "be subject for the Lord's sake to every human institution" (v. 13). Here, in words reminiscent of Paul's teaching in Romans 13, Peter has in mind, "the emperor as supreme, or to governors as sent by him to punish those who do evil and to praise those who do good" (vv. 13–14). This, of course, is an admonition to all Christians.

Second, Peter goes from the general to the specific and urges slaves to "be subject to your masters with all respect, not only to the good and gentle but also to the unjust" (2:18). He goes on to encourage believers who find themselves in this situation to suffer for righteousness, "for this is a gracious thing, when, mindful of God, one endures sorrows while suffering unjustly" (v. 19) This is a theme to which he will return in the apologetic passage.

Third, Peter urges wives, in like manner, to "be subject to your own husbands, so that even if some do not obey the word, they may be won without a word by the conduct of their wives" (1 Pet. 3:1). Here Peter's admonition calls for faith in the face of "anything that is frightening" (3:6). Peter will return to this theme as well in the classic apologetic passage.

Finally, Peter ends the section by returning to the general principle. Hence, we end where he began, with an admonition to all Christians, regardless of their circumstance, to live in quiet, humble submission and faith:

> Finally, all of you, have unity of mind, sympathy, brotherly love, a tender heart, and a humble mind. Do not repay evil for evil or reviling for reviling, but on the contrary, bless, for to this you were called, that you may obtain a blessing. For
>
> > "Whoever desires to love life
> >   and see good days,
> > let him keep his tongue from evil
> >   and his lips from speaking deceit;
> > let him turn away from evil and do good;
> >   let him seek peace and pursue it.
> > For the eyes of the Lord are on the righteous,
> >   and his ears are open to their prayer.
> > But the face of the Lord is against those who do evil."
> >   (1 Pet. 3:8–12)

This forgotten paragraph gives us an important lens through which to view Peter's instruction in the better-known apologetic text that follows. When we examine this paragraph closely, we discover the identity, attitude, conduct, and character that are assumed in the paragraph that follows. In other words, this forgotten paragraph gives more depth and texture to Peter's words in 3:15.

The Identity of the Apologist

The phrase "finally, all of you" makes it clear that Peter is now addressing all Christians regardless of circumstance. He is now summing up his teaching on submission and having gone from the general to the specific, he returns to the general. This is crucial to our understanding of the next paragraph as it removes any doubt as to who is responsible for engaging in apologetics. The idea that apologetics is for a select few must give way to the clear teaching of Scripture, which places the practice squarely at the feet of every believer.

This might come as a shock to some. It might surprise some budding apologists who have viewed themselves as members of the Christian version of the Navy SEALs, but it also might surprise those who have been glad that we have those specialists so they don't have to learn philosophy, physics, linguistics, logic, zoology and, well, theology! As I will demonstrate, however, the art and science of apologetics can and should be much simpler than that.

The Attitude of the Apologist

Having revealed the identity of the apologist, Peter proceeds to his attitude. The apologist's attitude should be marked by "unity of mind, sympathy, brotherly love, a tender heart, and a humble mind" (1 Pet. 3:8). Unfortunately, this is hardly what we have come to expect from apologists. We think of them more like Lieutenant Daniel Kaffee thundering away at Colonel Nathan Jessup in the famous "you can't handle the truth" scene from *A Few Good Men*. Yet Peter paints quite a different picture—a picture that is consistent with the theme of the entire section and, more importantly, with the character of Christ.

This, of course, is not to say that engaging in apologetics is always calm and peaceful. Jesus had several rather heated exchanges in his day (see, for example, Matt 3:7; 12:34; 23:33, 37; Luke 3:7). I am sure he even raised his voice from time to time, such as when he overturned the tables of the money-changers in the temple and drove them out (Matt 21:12; cf. Mark 11:15; John 2:15). However, he never sinned in his anger (Eph. 4:26), and his words were always appropriate for the occasion (Eph. 4:29). This is important to note in light of the current atmosphere of political correctness which often views any passionate exchange as a sinful act not befitting our "gentle" Savior.

The Speech of the Apologist

The attitude of the apologist is manifest in his speech: "Do not repay evil for evil or reviling for reviling, but on the contrary, bless, for to this you were called, that you may obtain a blessing" (1 Pet. 3:9). The Greek word translated *reviling* means "to speak in a highly insulting manner."[3] This, of course, is the opposite of speaking "blessing." Thus, Peter encourages believers to offer blessing in the face of insult. Further, he puts an even finer point on the matter of proper speech when, quoting Psalm 34, he urges, "Whoever desires to love life and see good days, let him keep his tongue from evil and his lips from speaking deceit."

This gives us a glimpse into the context wherein apologetics takes place. We should not expect those at enmity with God to be friendly toward his apologists. Jesus made this clear when he warned, "If the world hates you, know that it has hated me before it hated you" (John 15:18). Paul later confirms the veracity of the Lord's words, both in his own experience and in the conclusion drawn therefrom: "Indeed, all who desire to live a godly life in Christ Jesus will be persecuted" (2 Tim. 3:12). Yet Paul's admonition, like Peter's, is that we "bless those who persecute [us]; bless and do not curse them" (Rom.12:14).

The Character of the Apologist

Of course the identity, attitude, and speech of the apologist is rooted in Christian character: "For the eyes of the Lord are on the righteous, and his ears are open to their prayer. But the face of the Lord is against those who do evil" (1 Pet. 3:12).

The phrase, "those who do evil" is reminiscent of admonitions throughout the section. Believers are urged to "keep your conduct among the Gentiles honorable" (1 Pet. 2:12) and be mindful of the fact that governors are "sent by him to punish those who do evil and to praise those who do good" (v. 14). Even slaves are to bear in mind that it is to no avail "if, when you sin and are beaten for it, you endure" (v. 20) but it is of great benefit to "do good and suffer for it " since "this is a gracious thing in the sight of God" (v. 20). All of these reminders culminate in this final reminder that "the eyes of the Lord are on the righteous, and his ears open to their prayers." This, too, harkens back to Peter's warning to husbands who are urged to conduct themselves properly toward their wives, "so that your prayers may not be hindered" (3:7).

With this Peter concludes the section. But it is important to remember that his following instruction on apologetics grows out of his words to the believing community in this section. In fact, it is impossible to understand the next paragraph, and by extension, Peter's teaching on apologetics, without connecting it to this lost paragraph. Therefore, as we turn our attention to the more familiar passage, let us remember the identity, attitude, speech, and character of the apologist.

THE CRITICAL TEXT

We have seen the broader context of Peter's teaching on apologetics. However, before we get to 1 Peter 3:15, we must still examine the immediate context and its connection to what we have seen so far. In order to do that, we must look at the paragraph as a whole:

> Now who is there to harm you if you are zealous for what is good? But even if you should suffer for righteousness' sake, you will be blessed. Have no fear of them, nor be troubled, but in your hearts honor Christ the Lord as holy, always being prepared to make a defense to anyone who asks you for a reason for the hope that is in you; yet do it with gentleness and respect, having a good conscience, so that, when you are slandered, those who revile your good behavior in Christ may be put to shame. For it is better to suffer for doing good, if that should be God's will, than for doing evil. (1 Pet. 3:13–17)

It is obvious that Peter is continuing many of the themes he introduced in the previous section. However, what we usually do not see is the manner in which these sections define apologetics in general, and the apologist in particular. But that is precisely what Peter does. And he does so in the context of our righteousness. This idea of righteousness is critical to our understanding.

Our Righteousness Makes Us Strangers and Aliens

One of the obvious yet unstated realities in this passage is that those who follow Christ are outsiders. There is a definite "us vs. them," or better yet, "them vs. us" element here. We are outside the power structure that determines whose standard of righteousness will be enforced. As a result, our righteousness is considered inappropriate and unwelcome. We have already noted that Peter refers to believers as "sojourners and exiles" (1 Pet. 2:11). And his statement prior to that explains *why* we are such:

> But you are a chosen race, a royal priesthood, a holy nation, a people for his own possession, that you may proclaim the excellencies of him who called you out of darkness into his marvelous light. Once you were not a people, but now you are God's people; once you had not received mercy, but now you have received mercy." (2:9–10)

There is a real sense in which Christians, regardless of where their earthly citizenship may be, are a people within and among a people. I am an American (more specifically, a Texan, which is an entirely different animal, but there is neither time nor space to get into that). But I am constantly reminded that I have an invisible passport that unites me to another people—the people to whom Peter refers in the passage above. This people transcends geographical borders, socioeconomic strata, ethnic distinctives, or generational differences.

Nor are we the only ones who recognize this truth. As we sojourn among our fellow citizens and Christ is formed in us (Gal. 4:19), our Christian citizenship marks us as outsiders, sojourners, exiles. Sometimes, the result is favorable. In America, for example, enough cultural Christian residue remains for people to view Christianity favorably.

And even though there has definitely been a steady slide away from our Christian moorings, even our politicians give lip service to Christianity since it is still difficult for one to stand up and say, "I am an atheist," and get elected.

Nevertheless, even here that good will goes only so far. Eventually, our Christian citizenship manifests itself in ways that are irreconcilable with our non-Christian neighbors. When that happens, we face opposition, and sometimes persecution and suffering, all of which relate directly to our righteousness in Christ.

Our Righteousness Brings Opposition and Suffering

"Now who is there to harm you if you are zealous for what is good? But even if you should suffer for righteousness' sake, you will be blessed" (1 Pet. 3:13–14). With these ominous words, Peter introduces what is undoubtedly the best-known apologetics text in the Bible: the text from which we derive the word *apologetics*. It is therefore important to note the tone his words set as well as their connection to his overall theme.

Earlier in the epistle, Peter noted:

> For to this you have been called, because Christ also suffered for you, leaving you an example, so that you might follow in his steps. He committed no sin, neither was deceit found in his mouth. When he was reviled, he did not revile in return; when he suffered, he did not threaten, but continued entrusting himself to him who judges justly. He himself bore our sins in his body on the tree, that we might die to sin and live to righteousness. (1 Pet. 2:21–24)

It is important to note that Peter is talking about more than people thinking ill of us or calling us names. The analogy he draws here is the suffering of Christ in his death at the hands of sinful men. Nor were the Messiah's first followers spared similar fates. According to early records, Philip "was scourged, thrown into prison, and afterwards crucified." Matthew was "slain with a halberd in the city of Nadabah." Andrew was "crucified on a cross, the two ends of which were fixed transversely in the ground." Mark was "dragged to pieces by the people of Alexandria." And Peter himself, "was crucified, his head being down and his feet upward, himself so requiring, because he was (he said) unworthy to be crucified after the same form and manner as the Lord was."[4]

We know, then, that apologetics is not a tool to make people like or accept us. But that is precisely the way many of us engage the culture. It is as though we believe that if we just make the right argument, refute the right falsehood, and set forth the right set of facts, then people will bow the knee and surrender to Christ—or at least lay down their weapons and leave us alone. However, as Peter notes here, the opposite is actually more likely. Instead of being a tool that alleviates the tension between us and the world, apologetics is often a tool that heightens that tension. Nevertheless, we echo the words of Luther's great hymn:

> And tho' this world, with devils filled,
> Should threaten to undo us,
> We will not fear, for God hath willed
> His truth to triumph thro' us:
> The Prince of Darkness grim,
> We tremble not for him;
> His rage we can endure,
> For lo, his doom is sure,
> One little word shall fell him.[5]

Our Righteousness Is Born of Our Devotion to Christ

In words reminiscent of Isaiah, Peter urges: "But in your hearts honor Christ the Lord as holy" (1 Pet. 3:15). Peter is here adapting the prophet's words in Isaiah 8:13: "But the LORD of hosts, him you shall honor as holy. Let him be your fear, and let him be your dread." The context in Isaiah is informative, as Simon Kistemaker observes: "In his day, Isaiah told the people not to fear the invading Assyrian armies but to revere God. In his epistle, Peter has the same encouraging message."[6] In light of the context, it is clear that Peter is not calling for a mere spiritual devotion to Christ, though that is certainly in view, but a choice to honor Christ in a culture that opposes and even punishes such devotion.

Moreover, the reason for this choice is clear: Jesus is the Lord Almighty! Again, Kistemaker notes, "[Peter] changes [Isaiah's] wording by honoring Christ as the Lord Almighty, so that he is the Lord Christ."[7] Thus, the Christian does not merely choose Christ as one among many options. Instead, Christ is set apart, honored, and sanctified over and above those who would threaten us *because* he is the Lord. Here the words of Christ: "Do not fear those who kill the body but cannot kill the soul. Rather fear him who can destroy both soul and body in hell" (Matt. 10:28).

As we noted earlier, most Christians do not engage in apologetics due to fear. Now we see the true nature of this fear. Ultimately it is fear of man. We hold men and their approval (or fear of the consequences of their disapproval) in higher regard than we do the Lord, the Messiah, Jesus.

I need to be reminded of this frequently. I, like the rest of my brothers and sisters in Christ, have a tendency to seek the easy way out. I like to be liked. I don't like being considered out of touch or out of my mind by strangers whom I meet along the way. Therefore, unless I remind myself constantly of my need to "honor Christ the Lord as holy," I will end up honoring my reputation, or, worse yet, the opinions of men, as most prized and precious in my heart. The result is compromise that dishonors Christ *and* deprives my hearers of the greatest news they will ever know. Oh, how I need to sanctify Christ in my heart!

Our Righteousness Requires an Explanation

Peter assumes that the righteousness that sets us apart from a world without Christ will eventually raise questions in the minds of "the ungodly and the sinner" (1 Pet. 4:18). Hence, he adds, "Always being prepared to make a defense to anyone who asks you for a reason for the hope that is in you" (3:15). This is the essence of apologetics. We translate the Greek word *apologia* as "make a defense"; we derive our English word *apologetics* from *apologia*.

First, we must know what we believe. This is "the hope that is in you." This is the object and substance of your faith. Without this, there would be no reason for anyone to ask you anything about God or the gospel, since, without this, you would not be a Christian. "For in this hope we were saved" (Rom. 8:24).

Second, we must know why we believe it. Peter makes it clear that we are to have "a reason for the hope that is in us." We do not merely hope for hope's sake. We hope because we have come to believe. We have a reason to hope. This, of course, assumes that we have actually believed something. We are to be like Theophilus, whom Luke exhorted to "have certainty concerning the things you have been taught" (Luke 1:4).

Paul's words to Timothy are most helpful here. Repeatedly in his second epistle to the young man, Paul admonishes him to hold fast to the content, or "reason" for his faith. In the first chapter, he urges Timothy to "follow the pattern of the sound words that you have heard from me, in the faith and love that are in Christ Jesus. By the Holy Spirit who dwells within us, guard the good deposit entrusted to you" (2 Tim. 1:13–14). In chapter 2, Paul admonishes Timothy to pass what he has heard on to others: "What you have heard from me in the presence of many witnesses entrust to faithful men who will be able to teach others also" (2:2). And in the third chapter, Paul reminds young Timothy of the source of his hope when he urges, "Continue in what you have learned and have firmly believed, knowing from whom you learned it" (3:14).

Peter's words undoubtedly refer to the same content. There is a substance to our faith that goes beyond what we feel. It is tangible and measurable. It can be defined, memorized, and defended. The source is outside of us and available to all. It is the apostolic record of the person and work of Christ.

> Therefore we must pay much closer attention to what we have heard, lest we drift away from it. For since the message declared by angels proved to be reliable, and every transgression or disobedience received a just retribution, how shall we escape if we neglect such a great salvation? It was declared at first by the Lord, and it was attested to us by those who heard, while God also bore witness by signs and wonders and various miracles and by gifts of the Holy Spirit distributed according to his will." (Heb. 2:1–4)

Third, knowing what we believe and why is not enough. We must also be willing and able to explain that belief to others in a winsome manner. We must "always be prepared to make a defense." Technically, *apologia* means to give a verbal defense. It is actually a legal term. Essentially, a lawyer gives an "apology" in a courtroom. This definition captures the sense in which the defense is to be given. The goal is not merely to give information in a dispassionate manner; the goal is to convince. Hence, we must be winsome in our delivery. This, too, is a product of our righteousness.

Our Righteousness Shapes Our Explanation

Peter's words, "yet do it with gentleness and respect" (1 Pet. 3:15), were by far the hardest for me to incorporate in my thinking about apologetics. Until my last year in college, I had my sights set on practicing law. I was the classic young debater. I was always looking for a good verbal sparring match. My mind was sharp and my tongue was quick. I was absolutely merciless! However, what it took me a while to see was that (1) people didn't want to engage me after a while, and (2) my testimony was suffering. I needed desperately to be pulled aside and pointed to Peter's words. And that's exactly what happened.

Brent Knapton, one of my teammates on the football team at Rice University, was the most gentle man I knew. Yet he was as firm in his convictions as anyone. Brent saw my flaw and took me aside. Even the way he confronted me was an example of Peter's admonition to gentleness and respect. Thus, he not only told me; he showed me what Peter's words meant. When I am tempted on occasion to be less than gentle in my approach to those with whom I disagree, I still hear his words in my head.

As noted earlier, there is a difference between being firm or forceful in our approach, and exercising gentleness and respect. Gentleness is not a lack of strength; it is strength under control. Gentleness is me wrestling with my three-year-old daughter. *Respect*, on the other hand, is a word that can also be translated *fear*. However, it is not "seeking the approval of man" (Gal. 1:10). It is instead a fear or respect for God.[8] In other words, our defense should be given as though we are keenly aware that God is watching. Also, we must remember that "a soft answer turns away wrath, but a harsh word stirs up anger" (Prov. 15:1).

Our Righteousness Vindicates Our Explanation

Peter concludes this section with the admonition, "Having a good conscience, so that, when you are slandered, those who revile your good behavior in Christ may be put to shame. For it is better to suffer for doing good, if that should be God's will, than for doing evil" (1 Pet. 3:16–17). And so we end where we began. Remember, Peter opened this paragraph with the words, "Now who is there to harm you if you are zealous for what is good? But even if you should suffer for righteousness' sake, you will be blessed" (vv. 13–14). Now we have come full circle.

By framing the discussion with suffering on either side, Peter makes it clear that he is not offering a means by which Christians dominate discussions, overthrow empires, or change public opinion. Apologetics is ultimately an expression of our willingness to suffer rather than compromise. It is the explanation for our suffering, both in terms of why we suffer and how we suffer. Apologetics is our answer to those at whose hands we suffer as well as those who witness our suffering. Apologetics says to a watching world, "We have been captured by something so profound that we are willing not only to be considered fools, but to suffer as such."

"For Christ also suffered once for sins, the righteous for the unrighteous, that he might bring us to God, being put to death in the flesh but made alive in the spirit" (1 Pet. 3:18).

CONCLUSION

In this chapter, we have examined the identity, attitude, speech, and character of the apologist. We have also seen that our apologetic is rooted in a righteousness that is ours in Christ. We will see in the next chapter that the absence of this righteousness accounts for the unbelief of those who oppose us. While we proclaim the truth in the righteousness that is found in Christ, they suppress the truth in unrighteousness. As such, our next stop is the first chapter of Paul's epistle to the Romans.

3

Why Unbelief?

It's a familiar scene. You are engaged in a conversation with someone and the topic turns to religion. The person to whom you are speaking is quick to point out that, although he is quite "spiritual," he is not religious. You inquire as to what he believes, he gives you a halfhearted answer, and you begin to share your faith.

However, at each point, he presents an objection. First, he objects to religion as a whole, to which you respond with a well-reasoned answer. Next, he objects to the specific religion of Christianity. Again, you answer. Then he objects to the Bible, and, of course, you have a cogent, winsome answer. Eventually, you discover a pattern: you make a point, he makes an objection, you answer the objection, he ignores your answer and moves on to something else.

I call this the Cycle of Foolishness. The name stems from the biblical idea of answering the fool, and the frustration of dealing with such foolishness. The Bible acknowledges this cycle with one of the most confounding Proverbs: "Answer not a fool according to his folly, lest you be like him yourself. Answer a fool according to his folly, lest he be wise in his own eyes" (Prov. 26:4–5).

In the first instance, "After, or according to his folly, is . . . equivalent to recognizing the foolish supposition and the foolish object of his question."[1] In other words, "Do not accept the foolish supposition or object of the fool."

The *sic et non* here lying before us is easily explained; after, or according to his folly, is this second time equivalent to, as is due to his folly: decidedly and firmly rejecting it, making short work with it (returning a sharp answer), and promptly replying in a way fitted, if possible, to make him ashamed.[2]

THE SPIRAL OF UNGODLY UNBELIEF

"For the wrath of God is revealed from heaven against all ungodliness and unrighteousness of men, who by their unrighteousness suppress the truth" (Rom. 1:18). At first glance, these words may seem to have nothing to do with apologetics. However, a closer examination reveals that this verse not only touches on the topic of apologetics; it is actually one of the foundational principles upon which our approach to the topic rests.

Romans 1:18 informs us about man's spiritual condition in relation to the truth we are trying to proclaim. Here, Paul makes it clear that our hearers don't have an information problem; they have a sin problem. Of course, ignorance figures into the equation. However, at a fundamental level, ignorance is not their issue. They "suppress the truth" in their unrighteousness.

Paul's theme in Romans 1:18–3:20 is the universality of sin and condemnation. Murray notes, "It is to the establishment of this thesis that this whole passage is directed." Paul makes this clear "by reprising 1:17 in 3:21."[3] In 1:17 and 3:21 Paul references the fact that the just, or righteous, live by faith. Moo argues, therefore, that 1:18–3:20 should be seen "as a preparation for, rather than as a part of, Paul's exposition of the gospel of God's righteousness."[4]

This influences our strategy directly. If man's problem is a lack of information, then our approach in apologetics must be information-heavy. Our goal has to be finding the areas where the hearer is uninformed and informing him. Moreover, if his problem is an information problem, we can rely on the information to do the work of convincing and converting.

If, on the other hand, man's primary problem is a sin problem, then information alone is not sufficient. The answer to sin is not information, but repentance! Hence, we need to back up a couple of verses. In 1:16, Paul reminds us that the gospel is "the power of God unto salvation." In the next verse he connects that truth to the question of righteousness: "For in it the righteousness of God is revealed from faith for faith, as it is written, 'The righteous shall live by faith'" (v. 17). When we read in verse 18 of "men, who by their unrighteousness suppress the truth," our attention should be drawn back to the previous statement.

What, then, is the great need of those who suppress the truth in unrighteousness? The answer, according to verses 16 and 17, is the faith! *Therefore, we should never divorce apologetics from gospel proclamation.* To do so would be to (1) fail to meet our hearers' greatest need, (2) neglect the greatest tool at our disposal, and (3) ignore the spiral of ungodly unbelief.

Men Know God

The spiral of ungodly unbelief is the process whereby men go from the knowledge of God to the unabashed worship of idols. The spiral begins with God's revelation of himself to man. Paul presents this in Romans 1:19–20: "For what can be known about God is plain to them, because God has shown it to them. For his invisible attributes, namely, his eternal power and divine nature, have been clearly perceived, ever since the creation of the world, in the things that have been made. So they are without excuse."

Three phrases in this paragraph support Paul's conclusion that people are "without excuse" in terms of general revelation. First, the phrase, "is plain to them," reminds us that the knowledge of God we receive from general revelation does not require unusual effort. The second phrase, "God has shown it to them," reminds us that general revelation is not hidden or secret. The third phrase, "have been clearly perceived," reminds us that *general revelation* (Rom. 1:18–31) cannot be missed by accident. Doing so requires suppression.

Put these three together and we see that God has provided a means of knowing about him that requires no special effort, is not hidden, and cannot be missed unless, of course, we *want* to miss it. And *that* is why those who "miss it" are said to be "without excuse." Thus, the spiral begins when men reject God's general revelation. Consequently, they continue downward and refuse to honor the God they know.

Men Do Not Honor the God Whom They Know

Having no excuse does not necessarily make men sin. In the following chapters, Paul is going to point to the faithfulness of both Jews and Gentiles. In both cases, they were without excuse, but they ended up righteous as opposed to sinful. Why? Because they honored God. Those who continue downward on the spiral of ungodly suppression, on the other hand, go from bad to worse: "For although they knew God, they did not honor him as God or give thanks to him, but they became futile in their thinking, and their foolish hearts were darkened" (Rom. 1:21).

Men Become Fools

"Claiming to be wise, they became fools" (Rom. 1:22). The Greek word translated *fools* in this verse (*moros*) means "to become insipid; figuratively, to make as a simpleton."[5] It is the word from which we derive our word *moron*. The Bible literally says that men who deny God's existence are morons who are so foolish, they actually think they are wise. Or as my grandmother used to say, they're "educated fools." *The New International Theological Dictionary of New Testament Theology* adds, "*Moros* means foolish, stupid and, like *moria*, foolishness denotes inappropriate behavior, thought or speech, both of single lapses of sense as well as in the sense of a permanent attribute."[6]

In other words, people who claim to be wise apart from God are not just acting foolishly in the moment; they are demonstrating the lifestyle and worldview they have adopted, and the impact thereof. The idea behind the word *moros* is that there is "a power which dominates man."[7] His foolishness is beyond his comprehension or control. He acts foolishly, but believes that his foolishness is wisdom. This is a critical point for the expository apologist. We need to be aware of the fact that what sounds foolish to us sounds wise to our interlocutor. We must know that while we're asking ourselves, "Does she really believe this foolishness?" she is actually thinking, "Does he really believe this foolishness?"

Knowing this will impact both our expectations and our perspective. We need to know that we are dealing with fools—not in the sense that we look down on people or despise them, but in the sense that we recognize their blindness. Knowing this changes the way we define success. If I define success as being able to talk to people on their terms, then I will adopt foolishness as a starting point. However, if I define success as exposing and refuting the foolishness of the fool, then I will adopt God's truth as a starting point.

We also need to remember that we are dealing with people who believe *we* are fools. This will disabuse us of all notions of gaining "cool points" in the eyes of fools who think themselves wise as a direct result of their rejection of the one true God. Understanding the "folly" of God's wisdom to sinners (1 Cor. 1:25) is the essence of presuppositional apologetics.

Men Exchange the Glory of God for Idols

The manifestation of man's foolishness came in the form of idolatry as he "exchanged the glory of the immortal God for images resembling mortal man and birds and animals and creeping things" (Rom. 1:23). Clearly, this must be understood in light of God's command against idolatry in the Decalogue. The use of imagery like birds and animals and creeping things corresponds directly to the prohibitions in the second commandment:

> You shall not make for yourself a carved image, or any likeness of anything that is in heaven above, or that is in the earth beneath, or that is in the water under the earth. You shall not bow down to them or serve them, for I the LORD your God am a jealous God, visiting the iniquity of the fathers on the children to the third and the fourth generation of those who hate me, but showing steadfast love to thousands of those who love me and keep my commandments. (Ex. 20:4–6; cf. Deut. 5:8–10)

I will say more about this in chapter 7. For now, it's enough to say that God's universal, transcendent, perpetual moral law lay at the foundation of every aspect of man's downward spiral into ungodliness and unrighteousness. This is true in regards to both the first and second table of the law. Not coincidentally, Paul's statement about man's idolatry (the violation of the first table of the law) is followed by his explanation of man's unholiness (the violation of the second table of the law). Vertical sin becomes horizontal.

Men Indulge Their Lusts

It has been said, "We become what we worship." In fact, that is the title G. K. Beale chose for his *tour de force* on the subject of idolatry.[8] God created us as image bearers; we are made in his image to reflect his glory. When we turn that worship in another direction, we do not cease to be what we were created to be; we simply pervert the reflection. As we worship, we are conformed to the image of the one or ones to whom we give our allegiance, adoration, obeisance, time, talent, and treasure.

It makes sense, then, that as we continue in Romans 1, we read, "Therefore God gave them up in the lusts of their hearts to impurity, to the dishonoring of their bodies among themselves" (1:24), since this is a reflection of the idols to which man's attention is turned. And to remove any doubt as to why this happens, Paul adds, "*because* they exchanged the truth about God for a lie and worshiped and served the creature rather than the Creator, who is blessed forever! Amen" (Rom. 1:25). It is this exchange of true worship for idolatry that leads directly to man's indulgence of his ungodly lusts.

Men Shatter the Image They Bear

If the introduction of the idea of man's indulgence of his lust seems to imply sexual immorality as the chief means of expression, the next phase in the downward spiral leaves no doubt:

> For this reason God gave them up to dishonorable passions. For their women exchanged natural relations for those that are contrary to nature; and the men likewise gave up natural relations with women and were consumed with passion for one another, men committing shameless acts with men and receiving in themselves the due penalty for their error. (Rom. 1:26–27)

Unlike the previous statement, which pointed to a general indulgence in sexual sin, this reference points explicitly to homosexuality. Schreiner argues that this is due to the fact that homosexuality "functions as the best illustration of that which is unnatural in the sexual sphere."[9] Of course, this is a volatile statement in the contemporary political environment.

However, the facts are undeniable from a biblical, theological perspective. Homosexuality mars our view of the image of God by denying the complementary relationship between men and women. It denies procreation, one of the principal purposes for which God designed marriage and sex. It blasphemes the illustration of Christ's self-sacrificing love for his church. And it violates clear commands of Scripture. Hence, while all sexual sin is an expression of idolatry, homosexuality is a step further down the road of depravity. However, it is not the last step.

Men Lose Their Minds

The final phase in the downward spiral happens when men lose their minds and throw off all restraints. Having crossed the barriers of sexual morality, all other bets are off. The results? "And since they did not see fit to acknowledge God, God gave them up to a debased mind to do what ought not to be done" (Rom. 1:28).

Paul goes on to give practical examples of what it looks like when this final barrier is crossed:

> They were filled with all manner of unrighteousness, evil, covetousness, malice. They are full of envy, murder, strife, deceit, maliciousness. They are gossips, slanderers, haters of God, insolent, haughty, boastful, inventors of evil, disobedient to parents, foolish, faithless, heartless, ruthless. Though they know God's righteous decree that those who practice such things deserve to die, they not only do them but give approval to those who practice them. (Rom. 1:29–32)

The phrase "though they know God's righteous decree" is an obvious reference to the law of God. Again, Paul makes it clear that there is an objective standard involved here. Men are not merely doing things that are not profitable; they are violating the law. Nor is Paul's ire raised only against those who practice such immorality. In using the phrase "they not only do them but give approval to those who practice them," he makes it clear that failure to expose and/or condemn such action is equally vile in God's sight.

THE APOLOGETIC RESPONSE TO THE SPIRAL

Much more could be (and has been) said about this section of Romans. However, for our purposes, a few things are important to remember. First, it is important to remember that God has informed us of the true condition of our hearers. Men are not as rational as we think. No matter how "intelligent" you think your hearers are, God says they are fools. And they are not only fools; they are deceived fools who think they are wise. They are immoral fools who think they are righteous. Therefore, we must not be intimidated by them.

I frequently receive letters and e-mails that begin with, "I have a friend/parent/child who is extremely intelligent . . ." What follows is usually an impassioned plea for some kind of special apologetic methodology for the awesomely intelligent. It is as though we believe people who have studied science, philosophy, or mathematics stand on some lonely pedestal where not even the Holy Spirit can reach them. Suddenly, we believe Hebrews 4:12 reads, "The word of God is living and active, sharper than any two-edged sword, piercing to the division of soul and of spirit, of joints and of marrow, and discerning the thoughts and intentions of the heart . . . *unless, of course, the person is really smart!*"

Romans 1, however, reminds us that this is not the case. Men are not too wise for God—just too wise for their own good. Nor is the answer to their deception some special apologetic voodoo preserved especially for them. Don't be intimidated by the wisdom of men.

Second, remember that God has informed us of our hearers' greatest need. They may have questions that need to be answered. However, that is not their greatest need. Their greatest need is the gospel! The same gospel that saved you. The same gospel that saved Paul. The same gospel that is "the power of God for salvation to everyone who believes, to the Jew first and also to the Greek" (Rom. 1:16).

Any approach to apologetics that is not centered around the gospel is insufficient. What good does it do for me to convince a man that the earth is young if I don't convince him he is a sinner in need of a Savior?

What good does it do to reason with him in an effort to win him to "theism" if that theism remains undefined? What good does it do to convince a man that Jesus really lived if I don't tell him that Jesus really died and rose again? And what good does it do if I walk away from an interaction having won an argument, but lost a soul?

Nor am I proposing an either/or proposition. In each of these instances, I want both! I want to convince people that the earth is not billions of years old *as* I point them to the Creator and Lawgiver whose image they bear and whose law they've broken. I want people to see the truth of theism *as* I point them to the one true God. I want them to know the historicity of Jesus's life *and* his resurrection, as well as the implications of both for their life and eternity. In short, I want to win the person, not just the argument. And the only thing that can accomplish that is the gospel.

Third, remember that God has informed us of the likely response of our hearers. I am often amused as people ask me for ways to do apologetics that are least likely to offend lost people. It reminds me of one Mother's Day when I was riding in the car with my mother. We were driving down the street in our beat-up old Volkswagen Beetle when a police officer pulled us over.

The officer was very professional and even courteous. However, my mother was in a hurry. Besides, who wants to be pulled over by a cop? Eventually, he wrote her a citation, placed it in her hand, smiled, and said, "Happy Mother's Day." You would have thought he slapped her in the face! My mother went off. She started saying things I would never write in this book. I was terrified that the officer, who could obviously hear her, was going to come back and slap the cuffs on her.

Today we look back on that exchange and laugh. However, at the moment, it was anything but funny. But what was the officer supposed to do? The sheer fact of his presence was an irritant. The fact that he was hindering her only added to the irritation. And the fact that he gave her a citation, well, that was just icing on the cake. There was nothing he could have said to make that exchange less "offensive" to my mother.

Engaging in apologetics can often be like this. People are riding along enjoying their life when all of a sudden, here we come. We slow them down, tell them they're wrong, and offer correction. There is no way to do this without risking offense. In fact, just like the officer learned that day, our efforts to be sweet and polite can often be the very flame that lights the fuse on an already volatile situation.

We need to be aware that "the light has come into the world, and people loved the darkness rather than the light because their works were evil" (John 3:19). We need to be reminded of some of the most poignant words Jesus ever spoke:

> If the world hates you, know that it has hated me before it hated you. If you were of the world, the world would love you as its own; but because you are not of the world, but I chose you out of the world, therefore the world hates you. (John 15:18–19)

Attempting to be loved by the world often leads to compromise. As apologists, we do not wish to be more offensive than necessary. However, we know that there will be offense. We might as well offend with the gospel.

Finally, remember that God has informed us of the fate of our hearers. These are people who "deserve to die" (Rom. 1:32). This is not simply a reference to the Mosaic law and its civil penalties for the aforementioned sins. This is something far worse. These people deserve "the second death" (Rev 2:11; 20:6, 14; 21:8). These people deserve hell. And, lest we be puffed up with pride, this list in Romans 1:29–32 reminds us that we, too, deserve hell. The point here is to give us a sense of urgency, not superiority.

How, then, do we approach apologetics in light of these truths? It is the belief in the aforementioned realities that has led me to expository apologetics.

BELIEVE NO ONE WHO CALLS HIMSELF AN ATHEIST

If what Paul says is true, there is ultimately no such thing as an atheist. Anyone who calls himself one is wrong on at least three fronts. First, someone who claims to be an atheist is suppressing the truth he knows. According to Romans 1, "What can be known about God is plain to them" (v. 19), and their denial is an expression of the fact that they are among those "men, who by their unrighteousness suppress the truth" (v. 18). Therefore, whatever they believe about themselves, the God who made them says otherwise, and we must believe God rather than man.

Second, anyone who claims to be an atheist is contradicting the God of truth. It is one thing for a person to be wrong about himself. It is quite another thing for him to be in disagreement with what God says about him. God says every man knows. Therefore, anyone who says he doesn't know is calling God a liar. It's a bit like a man arguing with his mother about what day he was born. Only in this case, it's not his mother, but his inerrant, infallible, Creator.

Third, anyone who claims to be an atheist is ignoring his greatest need, and his only hope for its fulfillment. Man's greatest and ultimate need is God. Apart from God, man is incomplete. Moreover, he is utterly incapable of achieving or attaining what he lacks. This is what drove Solomon to write, "Then I considered all that my hands had done and the toil I had expended in doing it, and behold, all was vanity and a striving after wind, and there was nothing to be gained under the sun" (Eccles. 2:11). This is the state of every person apart from God.

REMIND PEOPLE OF WHAT THEY ALREADY KNOW

People know there is a God. As we have already seen, Paul makes it very clear that people know God exists. However, they suppress that truth in their unrighteousness. Nevertheless, the knowledge is within them. We see it in various ways in even the most ardent deniers of deity. (1) We see it in times of crisis, like the days following the tragedy of September 11, 2001, or December 7, 1941. (2) We see it in times of great joy, like the birth of a baby or the moment their team wins the big game. (3) We see it in times of fear, like when the Apollo 13 astronauts were in peril, or during the Cuban Missile Crisis. In times like these, men are well aware that God exists.

People know there is truth. Much has been written about post-modernism and its denial of absolute truth. However, even the most hardened truth-denier believes you should take him at his word. The oft-used example is the person who states, "There is no absolute truth," only to be faced with the response, "So you're saying truth exists and Jesus is Lord?" To which he will respond, "No, that's not what I said."

Of course, this admittedly simplistic example fails to capture the complexity of postmodernity. However, the point is clear: all people believe in truth. They prove this every time they make a statement that they expect others to understand.

People know there is right and wrong. One of the first phrases children learn to say with conviction is, "That's not fair!" We know in our bones that some things are just not right! Events like September 11, 2001, and December 7, 1941, stand as lasting reminders that there is a universal sense of right and wrong. On those days, people didn't stand around debating whether the Bible condemns murder; they just shouted, "That's not fair!" Ironically, many of them did so in direct opposition to the worldview they had embraced. Nevertheless, in moments like these, even fools become wise—at least for a moment.

People know they are not righteous. Shortly after we learn to say, "That's not fair!" we learn to say, "Nobody's perfect." This is our way of acknowledging our lack of righteousness without impugning ourselves. You see, if there is one who is perfect, then I am simply a sinner. However, if there is not one who is perfect, then I am no worse than anyone else, and, therefore, righteous by comparison. Of course, there *is* One who was and is perfect. Therefore, it is incumbent upon us to introduce those who have imbibed this falsehood to our perfect Savior.

People know judgment is necessary. On May 2, 2011, we discovered that an elite team of Navy SEALs had executed a predawn raid in Abbottabad, Pakistan, where they captured and killed Osama Bin Laden. Response to the news was almost universal, as people from all walks of life sighed in relief knowing that one of the most notorious terrorists in world history had faced swift justice.

Why do people respond this way? Why is the natural, visceral response one of almost universal approval of retributive justice? Because people know that judgment is necessary. They know that wrongs need to be set right. And if they know that, then they know, somewhere down deep in their own souls, that they, too, deserve justice for the sins they have committed. Of course, people suppress this knowledge in various ways, from appealing to others' worse behavior to judging ourselves by our intentions rather than our actions But the fact remains that we know better.

People know they need a Savior. The fact that people know they are guilty leads inevitably to the fact that they know they need a Savior. Again, people don't admit this. In fact, they suppress it. But they know it. Unwittingly, people will admit this knowledge in various ways. First, they will acknowledge their need for a Savior while claiming to be able to fulfill that role themselves. For example, the one who believes that he's "basically a good person," is essentially claiming to be able to make propitiation for his own sin. The same is true for the person who believes he has done good deeds that make up for his sins. In both cases, the person compounds his guilt by (1) acknowledging God's justice and the need for atonement while (2) elevating himself to the stature and status of God himself, "who is the Savior of all people, especially of those who believe" (1 Tim. 4:10).

The fact that people believe these things doesn't necessarily make our job easier. In fact, the hardest part of expository apologetics is convincing others of that which they already know. The tendency to "suppress the truth in unrighteousness" is not to be taken lightly or trifled with. People will fight tooth and nail against the aforementioned truths. However, there is a power greater than man, and it is that power on which we rely. This is why the expository apologist must say with the apostle, "I am not ashamed of the gospel, for it is the power of God for salvation to everyone who believes" (Rom. 1:16).

REFUSE TO MAKE THE FOOL GOD'S JUDGE

In addition to refusing to believe anyone who calls himself an atheist, and reminding people of what they know, we must also refuse to make the fool God's judge. There is a difference between answering the legitimate question of a peer or equal and presenting evidence to a judge. Expository apologetics takes these distinctions seriously. This is very important in light of the fact that the primary objection to this approach is that it reduces everything to Bible quotes and fails to take questions seriously. And if that is the way we operate, those who object are right to do so. However, the expository apologist must always take questions seriously and answer those he can. Nevertheless, there is a right and a wrong way to do that. The wrong way is to assume that man's greatest need is information. The right way is to remember that man's greatest need is illumination.

Assuming that man's greatest need is information leads to an approach to apologetics that seeks only to answer people's questions. The idea is that (1) people are asking legitimate questions, and (2) good answers will satisfy them and lead them to truth. This is usually wrong on both counts. First, people are rarely asking legitimate questions—or at least they are not asking the right ones. Frequently, their questions are mere smokescreens meant to stump you, make themselves sound more intelligent than they are, change the subject, or end the discussion. Rare is the person who has legitimate questions and is actually seeking legitimate answers.

Second, the fact that these questions are often illegitimate leads to the phenomenon I like to call "whac-a-mole apologetics." If you've ever been to an amusement park, you've probably seen the Whac-A-Mole game. This is where you take a big mallet and stand in front of a series of holes. When the game starts, moles pop up from the various holes and you have to whack them on the head before they disappear back from whence they came. Frequently, apologetic encounters resemble this game: People ask you a question, you answer, they shrug it off, and they ask another question. They don't acknowledge that you've just given them "evidence that demands a verdict," to quote Josh McDowell's legendary book. Instead, they move on, undaunted that you just demonstrated that their best reason for disbelief is a farce. That question merely disappears back into the hole from which it arose, and another question pops up in another location. And you just go on playing Whac-A-Mole as if they'll eventually run out of questions and bow the knee to Christ.

Unfortunately, this is not the way the game ends. This game ends much like the amusement park version. Time runs out, the moles stop popping up, and you've made no progress at all. This is about as frustrating as it gets for the apologist. However, there is another way. For the expository apologist, the goal is not just to whack the moles as they pop up. Our goal is to get to the gospel so that at the end of the "game" we are left with more than doubts as to whether we've wasted our time. We can know that when we rely on God's Word, we can also rely on the promise of him who said, "So shall my word be that goes out from my mouth; it shall not return to me empty, but it shall accomplish that which I purpose, and shall succeed in the thing for which I sent it" (Isa. 55:11).

Practically speaking, this is a matter of perspective. Do we believe that an apologetic encounter is an appeal to the mind of man, or to the Word of God? Do we believe that man is an impartial, all-powerful judge whom we must convince of the rightness and truthfulness of our claims? Or do we believe him to be a fool who suppresses the truth in unrighteousness, and will go on refusing to acknowledge the rightness and truthfulness of our claims "until the day dawns and the morning star rises in [his] heart" (2 Pet. 1:19)?

If the former is true, we will lay down our Bibles and try to convince our interlocutor of the rightness and truth of our claims by stepping out of our worldview and into his. We will say things like, "You can't use the Bible with people who don't believe it" and, "You've got to meet people where they are." The irony is that when we assume this posture, we essentially negate our claim to hold to a biblical worldview. We have agreed with our interlocutor that there can be truth apart from God. We agree with him that the Scripture is neither sufficient nor necessary. We have answered the fool and become "like him" (Prov. 24:4).

However, if the latter is true, we will hold on to the Scriptures, believing that God is the fountainhead of all knowledge and Christ is the repository of all wisdom and knowledge (Col. 2:3). We believe that "faith comes from hearing, and hearing through the word of Christ" (Rom. 10:17). As a result, like a warrior whose opponent does not believe in the existence of his sword, we refuse to lay down our arms and argue, opting instead to hack away, knowing that eventually, he will believe . . . or he will perish!

Nor do we simply quote Bible verses and ignore all questions. On the contrary, we answer! We answer just as though we were speaking *for* the Judge not *to* a judge.

DON'T TRY TO CURE UNRIGHTEOUSNESS WITH INFORMATION

Ultimately, what it all boils down to is what we believe man's true problem is, and where we go to find the solution. If man's problem is a lack of information, we rely on information alone. If man's problem is unrighteousness, we rely on the gospel. Expository apologetics definitely opts for the latter. Yet we still have to answer questions. And when doing so, we must remember to do three things.

1. *Answer honest questions.* The heart of apologetics is answering legitimate questions. After all, the apostle Peter defined apologetics as "always being prepared to make a defense to anyone who asks you for a reason for the hope that is in you" (1 Pet. 3:15). In the coming chapters, we will examine just what he meant by that. For now, suffice to say that he means for us to give answers to those who pose legitimate questions about what we claim to believe.

2. *Keep things simple.* There is a saying in diagnostic medicine: "When you hear hoofbeats, think horses not zebras." This is basically a reminder for doctors that, as Occam's razor states, the simplest answer is usually the best. Doctors shouldn't jump to the conclusion that they're dealing with the most exotic disease imaginable; they should start with the most likely one, because it's . . . most likely! The same is true for the apologist. Sometimes people will ask you about the origin of the universe because they are well read in PhD-level astrophysics and really do want to know if the Bible has answers to questions at the highest intellectual levels (zebra). However, more often than not, you'll be dealing with people who can't tell Darwin from Dickens, and wouldn't be able to understand a high-level explanation if you gave it to them (horses).

More importantly, both the horse and the zebra in this case need the same thing: the gospel! I may not be able to give PhD-level answers to astrophysics questions. However, that does not mean that I have nothing to say to a PhD in astrophysics. Remember Paul's word to the Corinthians:

> Where is the one who is wise? Where is the scribe? Where is the debater of this age? Has not God made foolish the wisdom of the world? For since, in the wisdom of God, the world did not know God through wisdom, it pleased God through the folly of what we preach to save those who believe. For Jews demand signs and Greeks seek wisdom, but we preach Christ crucified, a stumbling block to Jews and folly to Gentiles, but to those who are called, both Jews

and Greeks, Christ the power of God and the wisdom of God. For the foolishness of God is wiser than men, and the weakness of God is stronger than men.

For consider your calling, brothers: not many of you were wise according to worldly standards, not many were powerful, not many were of noble birth. But God chose what is foolish in the world to shame the wise; God chose what is weak in the world to shame the strong; God chose what is low and despised in the world, even things that are not, to bring to nothing things that are, so that no human being might boast in the presence of God. And because of him you are in Christ Jesus, who became to us wisdom from God, righteousness and sanctification and redemption, so that, as it is written, "Let the one who boasts, boast in the Lord." (1 Cor. 1:20–31)

3. *Always find a way to get to the gospel.* Sye Ten Bruggencate caused a great deal of consternation in the apologetic community with the publication of his video *How to Answer the Fool.* The controversy stemmed not only from his presuppositional approach, but from the fact that he criticized some of the best-known and respected apologists of our day or any other for their failure to "get to the gospel" in their interactions with unbelievers.

At one point, the video includes a clip of a well-known apologist answering questions after an hour-long lecture. During the Q&A, a young man objects to the apologist's "Christian assumptions," at which point the apologist fires back, "I never once mentioned Christianity. . . . I've only argued for theism." Bruggencate's response to this is dismay. How dare a Christian speak for an hour in front of an audience of unbelievers and not press the claims of Christ? How dare he fail to "get to the gospel!" Regardless of your take on Bruggencate's approach, it is hard to argue with him on this point . . . unless, of course, you subscribe to the notion that apologetics is only a precursor to evangelism, and that it is better to bring people closer to theism—which is closer to Christianity than atheism—than it is to alienate them altogether and risk losing a hearing by bringing the Bible and Christianity into the mix.

It is beyond the scope of this book to argue the strengths and weaknesses of various approaches to apologetics. However, make no mistake that I am arguing for an approach that refuses to leave the Bible behind. I am not assuming negative motives for those who travel other routes. Far be it from me to assume that I know all there is to know about apologetics. I am simply sharing the approach that I have come to view as the best and most accessible. My goal is to remove the barrier in people's minds that causes them to refuse to engage in apologetics because they view it as something beyond the reach of the average Christian. I want to promote and uphold the sufficiency of God's Word for apologetics.

I believe there is a place for high-level apologists who engage in discussion and debate with the academic world. However, I do not believe that doing so requires an abandonment of the Reformed, presuppositional approach. A classic example of this is James White. Dr. White is proficient in Greek, Hebrew, and Arabic. He is a New Testament scholar *par excellence!* He debates some of the biggest and brightest brains in the world. However, in doing so, he always gets to the gospel. I have seen him stand toe-to-toe with Muslims, atheists, Roman Catholics, Mormons, and homosexual activists, just to name a few, make high-level arguments worthy of the best New Testament critical scholars, and turn right around and press home the fact that the reason it all matters is because Jesus really is who the Bible says he is and he really did what the Bible says he did.

The goal of this book is not to turn us all into James White. Most of us don't have brains that big (present company included). However, we don't have to become James White in order to give an answer for the hope that is in us and point people to Christ. And that is exactly what men who suppress the truth in unrighteousness need more than anything else in the world.

4

Paul's Expository Apologetic

If expository apologetics is nothing more than a fancy gimmick I've invented, it is of little use to anyone. It will be difficult to understand, hard to remember, and impossible to place any faith in. If, on the other hand, expository apologetics is a biblical approach to dealing with objections, the story changes altogether. It will be much less complicated, easier to remember, and worthy of our faith. And, of course, we will be able to see examples of it in the Bible. That is why this chapter is so important. In this chapter, we will examine expository apologetics in action. More importantly, we will examine it in the New Testament.

Remember, expository apologetics is mainly about three things. First, it is about being biblical. We answer objections with the power of the Word. Second, it is about being easy to remember. If we can't remember this, we won't use it in our everyday encounters. Third, it is about being conversational. We must be able to share truth in a manner that is natural, reasonable, and winsome.

That is what makes the book of Romans a classic example of expository apologetics. On numerous occasions, Paul asks questions as though he were addressing an imaginary interlocutor. He then follows up with an answer to the question or objection. Some suggest that this is a mere rhetorical device. I beg to differ. The evidence suggests that Paul was not merely using a rhetorical device, but was actually answering questions that he had received from skeptics. I believe this for at least three reasons.

First, the questions he raises flow naturally. There is no sense of obscurity or disingenuousness in Paul's questions. They seem to flow as though they were part of a conversation. In fact, that's exactly what they were. As Paul preached the gospel, he encountered opposition. This opposition took the form of legitimate questions from people who were taken aback by the gospel Paul preached.

Second, the questions he raises are common. These questions are familiar to anyone who has discussed these issues with skeptics. In fact, on a number of occasions I have taken people to Romans and let them see the question they asked me in written form. I proclaim a biblical truth, the person with whom I'm speaking makes an objection, then I smile and say, Can I show you something? Amazing! Paul was most certainly in touch with the way people think and how they respond to the claims of the gospel. So much so that people are still asking the exact same questions.

Finally, if Paul had not heard these questions from others, he most certainly would have wrestled with them himself as a Jew embracing Christianity. As a Jew steeped in biblical thought, Paul did not easily receive the gospel message. He struggled to believe Christian claims. In fact, it was not until Christ confronted him in a powerful, personal way that the scales were removed from his eyes. Thus, while the form is clearly rhetorical, we have every reason to believe that Paul writes real answers to actual questions.

Remember, Paul is offering an apologetic for the gospel of Jesus Christ. He is preaching in a world where the death, burial, and resurrection of Jesus is still fresh in the minds of people. He is also preaching in a world where Jews and Gentiles don't mix, where Judaism still has a stronghold, and where Christianity is being maligned, syncretized, and persecuted. There is no written New Testament yet, the apostles are scattered, Christianity is growing in places far removed from its Jewish roots, and much of the church is in turmoil. This is not just some academic exercise. Paul is trying to make sure that the gospel is proclaimed and understood rightly. These questions, therefore, are crucial.

While we have the New Testament, and therefore are at a significant advantage, we still face syncretism. Christianity is still maligned. And in much of the world, the church is persecuted. There is even a movement afoot to go back to Judaism! I have met men and women who call themselves Christians, but have embraced much of the Levitical Code. They wear tassels on their clothes, hold to a Saturday Sabbath, keep kosher, observe feast days, refuse to shave their beards, use only God's Hebrew name, and more. Hence, these questions not only provide us a classic example of expository apologetics; they also provide us with very specific tools we can use as we engage our culture today.

APOSTOLIC ANSWERS TO EVERYDAY QUESTIONS

With that in mind, let's examine these classic questions to see what they teach us about the way the apostle Paul engaged in expository apologetics. The goal here is not an exposition of each passage. The goal here is to see and learn from Paul's pattern. Remember, we are looking for an approach that is biblical, easy to remember, and conversational.

Do Christians and Jews Get Saved in the Same Way?

The first question we encounter in Romans comes in chapter 3. There, after expounding on the guilt of the Gentiles before God in 1:18–32, then pointing his finger at the Jews in chapter 2, Paul starts the next section with a poignant question: "Then what advantage has the Jew? Or what is the value of circumcision" (Rom. 3:1)? If the Jews are as guilty as the pagans, what good is there in being a Jew? Paul likely faced this question on a number of occasions. And he is ready with an answer. His answer, however, is not as straightforward as you may expect.

Paul begins his answer in verse 2: "Much in every way. To begin with, the Jews were entrusted with the oracles of God." He then introduces three related questions before coming back to answer the main question more extensively in verses 10–18. Paul's response here is unique in that rather than quoting a particular Old Testament Scripture, he references Scripture as a whole. Then what follows is a series of three questions in rapid succession before he returns to the broader topic.

QUESTION 1: DOES MAN'S UNFAITHFULNESS
NULLIFY GOD'S FAITHFULNESS?

> What if some were unfaithful? Does their faithlessness nullify the
> faithfulness of God? By no means! Let God be true though every

one were a liar, as it is written, "That you may be justified in your words, and prevail when you are judged." (Rom. 3:3–4)

Note two things in Paul's response. First, he answers the questions in the negative. This is his usual practice. He asks what seems to be a rhetorical question, taking the tone and position of his interlocutor, then follows up with a negative response. It is as if he is saying, "I know what you are thinking, but you are wrong." His point is that our natural objections are the result of our suppression of truth in unrighteousness (3:18).

Second, he uses Scripture as the basis for his answer. Here he quotes Psalm 51:4. This is expository apologetics. He starts with a legitimate question, answers the question, and uses Scripture to shape and support his answer. Much can be said about and learned from Paul's use of the Old Testament. However, that is beyond the scope of this book. For now, we note that he engaged in expository apologetics.

Question 2: Are You Saying My Unrighteousness Is Good?

But if our unrighteousness serves to show the righteousness of God, what shall we say? That God is unrighteous to inflict wrath on us? (I speak in a human way.) By no means! For then how could God judge the world? (Rom. 3:5–6)

In the second question, Paul does not refer to Scripture, per se, as much as he refers to an accepted biblical principle: the fact that God is the judge of the world. But Paul is still engaging in expository apologetics since (1) his answer, though not quoting a particular verse, does come from the Bible, and (2) this question is a subset of a broader question to which he will return.

There is, however, something important we can learn here. A commitment to expository apologetics is not a commitment to quote book, chapter, and verse every time we make a statement or give an answer. Sometimes we refer to biblical truths in general. I make this point because it is easy to get caught up in the mechanics of this and forget the third criterion: it must be conversational! And while I long for the day when I am so conversant with Scripture that I speak normally, naturally, and effortlessly in book, chapter, and verse, I am not there yet! Nor do I have to be in order to engage in expository apologetics.

QUESTION 3: WHY AM I STILL CONDEMNED?

> But if through my lie God's truth abounds to his glory, why am I still being condemned as a sinner? And why not do evil that good may come?—as some people slanderously charge us with saying. Their condemnation is just. (Rom. 3:7–8)

Here, Paul uses the "I never said that" response. This is one of my favorites for a number of reasons. As a "cultural apologist," I tackle many hot-button issues. I don't shy away from divorce, same-sex "marriage," feminism, or evolution. Addressing some of these issues places me in the crosshairs of certain groups. I don't mind this; however, sometimes things can get ugly. I have been misquoted more than once, and accused of everything from hate crimes and misogyny to incest! That's right, I was once accused of incest by a feminist blogger who was trying to discredit me. The woman had never met me and knew absolutely nothing about me beyond what she heard in sermons or found online.

In this kind of environment, I have learned to be careful not only with what I say, but how I say it. Not that I back down from important cultural issues. I will never do that. However, I try to make it hard for adversaries to misrepresent my meaning. As such, I have developed an "I never said that" reflex. Sometimes I'll make a controversial point in a sermon, then I'll say, "Now you *did not* hear me say . . ." Hence, I am very fond of this particular Pauline response.

The idea here is that Paul's interlocutors are charging him with a form of antinomianism. There is, however, a fatal problem with their accusation: It is based on a faulty premise. Paul's gospel of grace did not nullify the law, as we shall see in his later response. As he unfolds his gospel, it will become clear that God takes righteousness very seriously—so seriously that Jesus would be:

> Put forward as a propitiation by his blood, to be received by faith. This was to show God's righteousness, because in his divine forbearance he had passed over former sins. It was to show his righteousness at the present time, so that he might be just and the justifier of the one who has faith in Jesus. (Rom. 3:25–26)

Thus, Paul argues that his accusers are not only wrong, but guilty of slander, and "condemned" for such an erroneous accusation (v. 8).

Paul does not answer this third question immediately. However, he does something else that is important for us to note. He is dealing with someone who is being dishonest, and he is calling him on it. This goes to the heart of our third goal. Remember, we want to be conversational, and conversations are two-way streets. In an honest conversation, it is sometimes necessary to call people out when they are being dishonest.

I do a lot of Q&A sessions at my events. In fact, it's one of my favorite things; it's the perfect setting to demonstrate expository apologetics. Of course, there is always the possibility of hostile or dishonest questions, and I have had my share of those. Usually, I just laugh it off, make a quick comment to let the people (and the audience) know that (1) I'm aware of what they're trying to do, and (2) I won't play along. However, sometimes people are either so persistent or so dishonest that I have to take a more direct approach.

I remember one instance when a man kept asking a question based on a false premise. He was a vehement anti-Calvinist who wanted to make a point more than he wanted to ask a question. His point was, "Calvinists believe all babies who die go to hell." Of course, this is not true. Nevertheless, no matter how many times I made that point, the man would come back with, "Well, if you guys believe all babies who die go to hell . . ." Again, I would respond, "No, sir, that is not what I believe." Eventually, after the third or fourth iteration of this, I simply stopped and said, "Sir, you are being dishonest. I have quoted our confession of faith, pointed you to books and statements by Calvinists, and given you my personal opinion on the matter. Right now you are simply refusing to believe anything other than the assumption you started with and are, therefore, being completely dishonest, even slanderous."

My goal was not to be mean; but to set the record straight and stop the advance of someone dead set on misrepresentation. This was important not only for the sake of those who were listening, but also for the sake of the man asking the question. If he was unwilling to let go of his assertion even after it was proven false, then we were not engaged in a conversation at all. This is part of the "answer a fool" strategy.

Recall this seemingly contradictory passage: "Answer not a fool according to his folly, lest you be like him yourself. Answer a fool according to his folly, lest he be wise in his own eyes" (Prov. 26:4–5). The first statement has to do with accepting the fool's false premise. The second has to do with disproving a fool's false premise. In other words, don't answer a fool's question unless and until you have exposed his folly.

Back to the Beginning

Paul then returns to answer his first question, "What then? Are we Jews any better off? No, not at all. For we have already charged that all, both Jews and Greeks, are under sin" (Rom. 3:9). And, as expected, he then runs straight to Scripture to shape and support his answer. What follows in verses 10–18 is a series of quotes from Psalms 14:1–3; 53:1–3; 140:3; 10:7; Proverbs 1:15; Isaiah 59:7–8; and Psalm 36:1. In rapid succession, Paul explains his understanding of man's sinful condition straight from Scripture. This, indeed, is classic expository apologetics.

Paul is being scriptural and conversational. And he is doing it from memory. This is not a formal debate or a wooden exchange. Paul's mind is ablaze with the Word of God, and he has a passion to preach the gospel. It is only natural for him to answer objections to the radical message he preaches. Nor is this an isolated incident. If we continue on in Romans, we will find more examples of Paul's approach to expository apologetics.

What Is the Christian's Relationship to the Law?

Then what becomes of our boasting? It is excluded. By what kind of law? By a law of works? No, but by the law of faith. For we hold that one is justified by faith apart from works of the law. (Rom. 3:27–28)

For what does the Scripture say? "Abraham believed God, and it was counted to him as righteousness." (Rom. 4:3)

Or is God the God of Jews only? Is he not the God of Gentiles also? Yes, of Gentiles also, since God is one—who will justify the circumcised by faith and the uncircumcised through faith. Do we then overthrow the law by this faith? By no means! On the contrary, we uphold the law. (Rom. 3:29–31)

If we are arguing that Paul is using Scripture to shape and support his apologetic, then we should find an Old Testament reference nearby. And, of course, we do. In the very next chapter, he introduces Abraham as his example: "What then shall we say was gained by Abraham, our forefather according to the flesh?" (Rom. 4:1). He goes on to quote Genesis 15:6 in support of his argument: "Is this blessing then only for the circumcised, or also for the uncircumcised? For we say that faith was counted to Abraham as righteousness. How then was it counted to him? Was it before or after he had been circumcised? It was not after, but before he was circumcised" (vv. 9–10).

CAN WE JUST LIVE ANY WAY WE WANT?

What shall we say then? Are we to continue in sin that grace may abound? By no means! How can we who died to sin still live in it? (Rom. 6:1–2)?

At first glance, Paul's answer appears not to conform to the expository apologetic pattern described above. Earlier, he referenced specific passages of Scripture. Here, his answer is not a direct quote. However, there is another theological issue we must consider.

Paul was an apostle (Rom. 1:1). That meant he was entrusted with unique authority and responsibility as one of Christ's messengers (Heb. 2:1–4). Paul's role as an apostle meant that what he was writing had the authority of Scripture. In other words, Paul's apostleship meant that he *was* in fact using Scripture. Jesus, the Word made flesh (John 1:1, 14), called to himself a number of apostles who would record, write, and preach what he taught. Although Paul's apostleship was unconventional (see 1 Cor. 15:8–11), he was an apostle nonetheless. His message was verified by his fellow apostles on two occasions (Gal. 1:18–2:2), and his writings were even referenced by the apostle Peter (2 Pet. 3:15–16). Therefore, it is safe to say that although Paul did not reference book, chapter, and verse in the Old Testament, he *was* citing what would eventually become known as the New Testament, and was, therefore, practicing expository apologetics.

The point we should remember here is that Paul's approach to apologetics was not dependent solely upon his ability to comprehend and interact with random facts. Instead, he was dependent upon God's revelation as his primary and ultimate source of authority. Nor is this to say that there were never times when he made reference to truths revealed elsewhere, or that we are prohibited from doing the same.[1] However, we must bear in mind that those things must always be on the periphery of our approach to apologetics as opposed to the center. Scripture must always remain at the center.

The apostle employs this same approach in answering objections to a host of other issues, including:

What then? Are we to sin because we are not under law but under grace? By no means! (Rom. 6:15)

What then shall we say? That the law is sin? By no means! (Rom. 7:7)

Did that which is good, then, bring death to me? By no means! (Rom. 7:13)

What then shall we say to these things? If God is for us, who can be against us? (Rom. 8:31)

What shall we say then? Is there injustice on God's part? By no means! (Rom. 9:14)

You will say to me then, "Why does he still find fault? For who can resist his will?" (Rom. 9:19)

How then will they call on him in whom they have not believed? And how are they to believe in him of whom they have never heard? And how are they to hear without someone preaching? (Rom. 10:14)

I ask, then, has God rejected his people? By no means! (Rom. 11:1)

So I ask, did they stumble in order that they might fall? By no means! (Rom. 11:11)

We can easily see "that this plausible and formidable objection to the apostle's doctrine is precisely the one that is commonly and confidently urged against the doctrine of election today. There would be no room for either this objection or the one in verse 14 if Paul had merely said that God chooses those whom he foresees will repent and believe, or that the ground of distinction is in the different conduct of men. It is very evident, therefore, that Paul taught no such doctrine. How easy and obvious an answer to the charge of injustice would it have been to say, God chooses one and rejects another according to their works. But teaching as he does the sovereignty of God in the selection of the subjects of his grace and of the objects of his wrath, declaring as he does so plainly, that the destiny of men is determined by his sovereign pleasure, the objection (how can he yet find fault?) is plausible and natural."[2]

Clearly, the apostle Paul engaged in expository apologetics. He was very adept at answering objections with the power of the Word. He took objections seriously, answered them directly, and always got to the gospel. He also did so in a cogent, winsome, conversational manner. However, he did not always use the exact same methods.

ACTS 17: A DIFFERENT APPROACH FOR A DIFFERENT AUDIENCE

While the book of Acts is very different from Romans in terms of genre, it still gives us a glimpse into Paul's expository apologetic. Unlike Romans, Acts is a travelogue. Luke gives the reader an overview of Paul's ministry. As such, it is difficult to pinpoint Paul's specific use of the techniques highlighted above. However, there are areas in Acts where Paul's approach to apologetics is clear—none more so than chapter 17, where we find his "Mars Hill" sermon.

Among the Jews

In Acts 17, two features are worth noting in light of our current discussion. First, the contour of the chapter allows us to see the difference between Paul's approach to apologetics with a Jewish audience, and the approach he took with Gentiles. In the first part of the chapter, Paul is in Thessalonica, where:

> There was a synagogue of the Jews. And Paul went in, as was his custom, and on three Sabbath days he reasoned with them from

the Scriptures, explaining and proving that it was necessary for the Christ to suffer and to rise from the dead, and saying, "This Jesus, whom I proclaim to you, is the Christ." (Acts 17:1–3)

No doubt his interactions with the Jews in Thessalonica were similar to his approach in Romans. Note that Luke says it "was his custom." Paul's expository apologetic in Romans dealt with the most basic questions with which his Jewish audience would surely have wrestled. Moreover, his extensive use of the Old Testament would have been a tremendous asset in the Jewish community of Thessalonica and beyond.

Note also that he (1) "reasoned with them from the Scriptures" and (2) got to the gospel. These are hallmarks of expository apologetics. Thus, it is reasonable to assume that Paul's expository apologetic would have been largely the same. However, this does not prove that Paul would use such an approach with a Gentile audience. Nor does it show us how, if at all, his approaches to the two audiences would differ. For that, we have to examine Paul's interaction in Athens.

Among the Gentiles

After another set of encounters with Jews in Berea, Paul headed to Athens. There, he resumed his practice of reasoning with the Jews in the synagogue. However, he also engaged with Gentiles in the marketplace (v. 17), including "some of the Epicurean and Stoic philosophers" (v. 18). It is here that Paul employs an abbreviated version of expository apologetics, a version with which modern Christians must be acquainted.

In Acts 17:22–33, Paul is dealing with a very different audience from the one he addressed in the epistle to the Romans. In Romans, he was writing to brothers and sisters who understood and believed the Bible; in Athens, he was dealing with pagans. This is important to note because the chief objection people have to expository apologetics today is that it is pointless to bring Scripture into discussions with people who do not believe the Bible.

However, we must bear in mind that our job is to answer questions about why we believe what we believe. That, after all, is the heart of apologetics (1 Pet. 3:15). And if what we believe is based on God's revelation, we cannot avoid referring to it in our answers—Paul certainly doesn't avoid it.

But we should pay attention to the differences between Paul's approach in Acts 17 and his approach in Romans. First, even a cursory reading of Acts 17 makes it clear that Paul is not using Scripture in the same way that he did in Romans. Here, Paul does not quote the Old Testament explicitly. The Romans passages were filled with reference after reference and quote after quote from the Old Testament. Not so in Acts 17.

Second, in Acts 17, Paul quotes one of *the pagans'* philosophers. Because of this, many conclude that Paul's approach to apologetics was more in line with those who abandon Scripture altogether. But he was simply trying to identify with his audience and meet them on ground that was familiar to them. And if Paul did this, how much more should we!

Having acknowledged the differences, we should understand that several key aspects of Paul's presentation in Athens are reminiscent of his approach in Romans. So reminiscent, in fact, that I argue he is still engaging in expository apologetics. First, although he does not quote the Old Testament, he does refer to its content. Paul's references to the creation account are biblical.

Second, in referring to the death, burial, and resurrection of Jesus, Paul is referring to the gospel. This is important since the gospel is at the center of New Testament Scripture. Thus, it could be said that Paul *is* using Scripture explicitly. He and his fellow apostles referred consistently to these same elements of the gospel in their teaching and writing. It was prevalent in their letters to the churches. In other words, it became Scripture.

Finally, rather than avoid biblical truth in this Mars Hill sermon, Paul overtly references biblical truth. Remember, the question here is whether we need to leave the Bible out of our discussions and meet people solely on their grounds. Paul's presentation leaves no doubt as to his preference in the matter. He uses a classic presentation of redemptive history following the pattern of creation, fall, redemption, and consummation.

CREATION

The bulk of Paul's presentation addresses the first of these four critical movements in the story of redemption: creation. After observing the Athenian culture and worship practices, Paul proceeds to reveal to them that which they worshiped in ignorance (Acts 17:23). To do so, he went straight to the creation account:

> The God who made the world and everything in it, being Lord of heaven and earth, does not live in temples made by man, nor is he served by human hands, as though he needed anything, since he himself gives to all mankind life and breath and everything. And he made from one man every nation of mankind to live on all the face of the earth, having determined allotted periods and the boundaries of their dwelling place, that they should seek God, and perhaps feel their way toward him and find him. Yet he is actually not far from each one of us, for "In him we live and move and have our being"; as even some of your own poets have said, "For we are indeed his offspring." (Acts 17:24–28)

That Paul is referencing the Genesis account can hardly be questioned. First, he calls God the "Lord of heaven and earth." This is obviously an allusion to Genesis 1:1. He then notes that this God "made from one man every nation of mankind to live on all the face of the earth." This, of course, is a reference to Adam. Both points are crucial to our approach to expository apologetics.

As noted before, expository apologetics does not necessarily require direct quotes from Scripture. In this case, Paul obviously alludes to the biblical narrative without directly quoting it. However, there is no question as to the origin of his worldview. This is important to bear in mind as we encounter people who question us at any point, but particularly those who question our beliefs about human origins. If we made a reference similar to the one Paul makes here, our audience would know that we reject the concept of atheistic evolution and believe in a personal God who created everything. Moreover, if we, like Paul referenced "one man," we would be indicating our belief in the biblical Adam.

This is a far cry from laying down the Bible to address those with a differing worldview. This is a frontal assault on a culture that did not share Paul's biblical understanding of creation. In fact, Paul's opening salvo is a no-holds-barred expression of, "You are wrong, and I'm about to set you straight." Nor did he stop there. He took things further by addressing the question of what men "ought" to do in light of the truth of creation.

FALL

When Paul uses the word ought, he is introducing the Athenians to the concept of sin. Make no mistake about it, he is accusing them of sin. Particularly, he is accusing them of the sin of idolatry. He continues:

> Being then God's offspring, we ought not to think that the divine being is like gold or silver or stone, an image formed by the art and imagination of man. (Acts 17:29)

Clearly, this is a reference to the second commandment. Perhaps in a Jewish environment Paul would have quoted the text. However, here, addressing an audience that would have been unfamiliar with Exodus 20, he merely states the truth contained in the text.

Paul is not just challenging his hearers to reevaluate their belief about God. Nor is he content with merely making a strong case for the reasonableness of his truth claims. He is pressing the claims of Christ and exposing sin. Again, this is at the heart of expository apologetics.

REDEMPTION

Paul makes it clear that this unbelief is a matter of sin by introducing the idea of repentance in the next verse:

> The times of ignorance God overlooked, but now he commands all people everywhere to repent. (Acts 17:30)

Nor is this repentance isolated to a particular people with a particular predisposition. This repentance is for "all people everywhere." If there was any question as to whether Paul was bringing sin into the equation, verse 30 answers it unambiguously.

CONSUMMATION

The final link in the redemptive chain is consummation: the idea that God will bring all things to a conclusion that manifests his glory through the redemption of his elect and the punishment of the wicked. The world will not go on without end. A day of reckoning is approaching:

> Because he has fixed a day on which he will judge the world in righteousness by a man whom he has appointed; and of this he has given assurance to all by raising him from the dead. (Acts 17:31)

Here, Paul returns to the heart of the gospel, and the most controversial aspect of his preaching. Earlier in the chapter Luke notes the response to Paul's preaching when he quotes them as saying, "'He seems to be a preacher of foreign divinities'—because he was preaching Jesus and the resurrection" (Acts 17:18).

There is no doubt that Paul preached the gospel to his Gentile audience without compromise. Moreover, having received negative feedback from his prior audience, Paul did not shy away from reiterating the heart of his message at Mars Hill. Far from avoiding this topic, Paul reserves it for the crescendo of his argument: "Now when they heard of the resurrection of the dead, some mocked. But others said, 'We will hear you again about this'" (Acts 17:32).

As noted earlier, this is the endgame of expository apologetics. The goal of connecting with our audience is always a servant of the greater goal of getting to the gospel. As we shall see later, it is very important to have a finger on the pulse of one's culture. Paul was a master and model of this. However, he was never relevant for relevance's sake. Nor did he withhold offensive or unpopular themes in an effort to preserve his credibility.

We need to keep this important truth in mind for at least two reasons. First, we live in an age that is as opposed to the idea of the gospel as first-century Athens. Our Epicurean and Stoic philosophers only differ from those to whom Paul preached in that they are not nearly as open to opposing ideas—especially ideas that (1) question their hegemony and (2) proclaim the resurrected Christ. The men of our day are intolerantly tolerant. In other words, they tolerate everything *but* intolerance. More accurately, they tolerate anything that doesn't threaten their hegemony.

Second, it is important to keep this truth in mind because, as we've noted, the modern idea of the apologist is that of the man-about-town; "the debater of this age" (1 Cor. 1:20). He is the person who can go toe-to-toe with agnostic or atheist philosophers for hours on end, never once quoting or even referring to a Bible verse, and bragging about the fact that he did so! He is the person who complies with the command of the moral relativist who says, "If you want to argue for your position in the modern, secular marketplace of ideas, you have to do so with arguments that have no basis in religion." It is hard to reconcile the expository apologetics we see Paul engaging in with the goals and norms of "polite Christian society."

Nevertheless, it is the apostle, not the philosopher, debater, or sage, who serves as our example. The apostle, with one finger on the pulse of the culture and another pointing squarely at the Word of God, is our guide. The learned Benjamite, the Roman citizen, the graduate of the University of Gamaliel, the one who "decided to know nothing among you except Jesus Christ and him crucified" (1 Cor. 2:2), is our model of the expository apologist.

TURNING THE CORNER

As we look ahead to the practical application of the themes examined thus far, it will be important to remember the lessons learned from both Romans and Acts. We must remember that men believe in God, and that they suppress that belief in unrighteousness. We must remember that our goal is to know what we believe and why we believe it, and to be prepared to communicate that in a natural, cogent, winsome manner. And we must remember that our ultimate goal is to get to the gospel. We are not in this to get people to abandon sections of their worldview while leaving their shaky foundation and infrastructure intact. Our goal is to lead people to the truth that will demolish the whole thing from the ground up!

To that end, we now turn our attention to the tools of the trade. From here on out our goal is to put these truths into practice. First, we will examine the foundation of our belief and the foundation of our discipleship. After that, we will turn to the importance of the moral law as the source of both the culture's criticism and our defense in cultural apologetics, and the Ten Commandments as the basis for our moral argument. Then we will explore the mechanics of expository apologetic encounters, and ways we can apply them to our preaching, teaching, and disciple making.

5

Learning Apologetics through Creeds, Confessions, and Catechisms

We are working with two definitions of apologetics, one broad, the other more narrow. Both definitions, however, help us understand the limited nature of our task. If, as Van Til argued, apologetics is vindication of the Christian world and life view against all others (the broad view), and we are commanded to know what we believe and why we believe it, and to always be prepared to communicate that to others in an effective, winsome manner (the narrow view), then the scope of our task is limited.

For example, when a Muslim asks me why I believe that Mary is the divine mother of God and the third person of the Trinity, I am under no obligation to defend that belief, since it is not what I hold to be true. Similarly, if I am asked to defend my belief in deceased relatives serving as guardian angels, universal salvation, or salvation based on a mere incantation followed by a life of wickedness (all of which I have heard numerous times), I can simply say, I don't believe that. I don't have to give an account for the beliefs of cults and heretics. I don't have to explain the convictions of the Word of Faith Movement, or the doctrines of the charismatic movement, the Church of Rome, or even paedobaptists. I am only responsible for giving a reason for the hope that is in *me*, not the hope that is in others.

Nor am I responsible for knowing what God has not revealed. For example, it is not necessary for me to know where babies go when they die, why God allowed the fall, or why mosquitoes exist! I have opinions about all of these. However, those things are not the reason for the hope that is in me. My hope is centered on the gospel of Jesus Christ. I am glad to have an honest discussion with a brother or sister who is really interested in the implications of these and other questions. However, with a person who is questioning the validity of Christianity, answers to these questions do him little good. Nor are these usually the question they *really* want to ask.

THE LIMITED NATURE OF OPPOSITION TO THE GOSPEL

The gospel has not changed over time. The message has remained constant from the time of Jesus to our day. Therefore, the objections to the gospel have not changed. People are asking the same questions today that were asked of Jesus and the apostles. There may be different nuances, but the core issues are the same. Thus, if we familiarize ourselves with the basic categories of questions and the key biblical texts that address them, we will be well equipped to engage in expository apologetics.

Several years ago, I had the privilege of addressing students at Oregon State University. I was there primarily to address several Christian groups that organized the meeting. However, one of the events was open to the general student body. It was presented as an opportunity to "Come Hear Dr. Voddie Baucham Discuss the Validity of the Bible." There were fliers up all over campus inviting students to come hear me give an address in the student center, followed by Q&A.

The fliers were simple and small. They had a picture of me and the basic information. I remember thinking to myself, "Nobody is going to show up for this!" When the time drew near, I found a quiet room where I could gather my thoughts and prepare (both for the smattering of attendees and for the comfort I was sure I would need to offer to the students who organized this flop). When the moment to begin arrived, one of the students came to get me. His demeanor was an awkward mixture of excitement and fear. And when I emerged from the room, I understood why.

The place was packed! There were students in every corner of the room. They sat on the floor, stood against the wall, and gathered just outside the main room. I couldn't believe my eyes. I contained my surprise, gathered my thoughts, and began to address the crowd. I lectured for nearly an hour, then opened the floor for questions. And that's when the fun really began.

Most college crowds in the Bible Belt produce questions designed to make the questioner look good. They want to stump the speaker, wax eloquent, or show off their knowledge. However, the Pacific Northwest proved to be quite different. First, most of the students were not Christians. There were Muslims, Hindus, Jews, Druids, Wiccans, and a few students who identified themselves simply as pagans. Nor were their questions like those I had come to expect from college students. These kids really wanted to know what Christianity was all about.

I took questions for over an hour. At the end, the students who had organized the event were astonished. They could not believe that I was able to stand firm and take any and all questions. They could not imagine how much I must have studied. Then I let the proverbial cat out of the bag. I told them that they could all do what I did if they would just become familiar with a few key concepts and a few key texts.

Of course, this is not to say that apologetics is easy. On the contrary, it requires a great deal of work. Knowing where to invest that work is key. And here is where expository apologetics takes a unique turn. When most Christians think *apologetics training*, they think philosophy, logic, and debate. However, the key tools for training the expository apologist are creeds, confessions and catechisms.

CREEDS: THE EARLIEST APOLOGETICS

If apologetics is about knowing what we believe and why we believe it, then the first place to start with our preparation is with our ancient creeds and confessions of faith. Christians have always been creedal people. Ironically, there are those who object to this fact. Many of my fellow Southern Baptists, for example, are fond of sayings like, "No Creed but Christ!" and "No Creed but the Bible." One needs only a slight grasp of logic to conclude that these are, in fact, creeds. But that never seems to stop anyone. Nor does the fact that both Mormons and

Jehovah's Witnesses can sign on to both of those statements and remain heretical. But I digress.

Ancient creeds are the wellspring of apologetic thought for at least three reasons. First, they were and are apologetic in nature. They are statements of belief written by early believers in response to heresy and/or opposition to biblical truth. They are reasoned responses to those questioning "the hope within us." Second, they are summaries of the gospel. They are statements designed to convey not only what the gospel is, but what the gospel is not. Third, these creeds are almost poetic in nature, and, therefore, easier to remember. This, of course, is one of the basic elements of expository apologetics.

Three creeds, in particular, have been helpful to me in my development as an expository apologist: the Apostles' Creed, the Nicene Creed, and the Athanasian Creed.

The Apostles' Creed

Over the years, the Apostles' Creed (written in the third and fourth centuries) has come to the fore in contemporary Christianity through the vehicle of song. I admit, I am not a fan of contemporary Christian music. However, I am always excited to see God's people being awakened to his truth in unique and diverse ways. This is especially true in a time rife with heresy and error. Interestingly, the creeds were tools meant to protect the church from such heresy.

> I believe in God the Father Almighty,
> Maker of heaven and earth.
> And in Jesus Christ, his only Son, our Lord;
> Who was conceived by the Holy Ghost,
> Born of the Virgin Mary,
> Suffered under Pontius Pilate,
> Was crucified, dead, and buried;
> He descended into hell [lit., *Hades*];
> The third day he rose again from the dead.
> He ascended into heaven
> and sitteth on the right hand of God the Father Almighty.
> From thence he shall come to judge the quick and the dead.
> I believe in the Holy Ghost,

the holy catholic church,
the communion of saints,
the forgiveness of sins,
the resurrection of the body,
and the life everlasting. Amen.

This is a summary of the gospel we preach! Why do we need to reinvent the wheel? This creed gives us at least three advantages in expository apologetics. First, it is historic. That means that we are able to explain to our interlocutors that this is not some esoteric idea we've come up with on our own, but it is the heritage of saints through the ages. Remember, our goal is to demonstrate not only that we have truth on our side, but that the ones whom we are engaging are arguing from a vacuum, a void. They are relying on their own fallen mind to determine what is true.

Second, it is easy to memorize. Remember, our goal is to be ready. As such, we want to rely on things we can call to mind at a moment's notice. The Apostles' Creed is a mainstay in liturgical churches, and used to be recited by believers of all stripes each and every Lord's Day. Even the smallest children knew this creed! As such, we know that memorizing it is not too much to ask of ourselves.

Third, the Apostles' Creed is available everywhere. I love being engaged in a discussion with someone about the claims of Christ and being able to point them to something they can go and look up on their own time. Often our encounters are limited. We've only got a few moments. And, while we should always point people to Scripture, it is not a bad idea to point them to something a little less daunting. After all, the Bible is huge!

The Nicene Creed

The Nicene Creed (AD 325; revised at Constantinople in 381) is very similar to the Apostles' Creed. However, it has a different emphasis. For example, the Apostles' Creed mentions the members of the Trinity but does not make the nature of their relationship to one another explicit. This is not to say that third and fourth-century Christians did not understand or believe in the Triune God. On the contrary, it is quite clear that they did. More importantly, it is quite clear that this is what the Scriptures teach. However, the authors of the Apostles' Creed were merely attempting to meet the needs of their day.

The Nicene Creed addresses a heresy that was common in its day and in ours: Arianism. Arianism espoused that Jesus is not divine, but that he is a created being. This heresy is behind the beliefs of groups like the Jehovah's Witnesses. James Robertson, in his *Sketches of Church History*, outlines the events surrounding the development of the Nicene Creed:

> There was a great deal of arguing about Arius and his opinions, and the chief person who spoke against him was Athanasius, a clergyman of Alexandria, who had come with the bishop, Alexander. Athanasius could not sit as a judge in the council, because he was not a bishop, but he was allowed to speak in the presence of the bishops, and pointed out to them the errors which Arius tried to hide. So at last Arius was condemned, and the emperor banished him with some of his chief followers. And, in order to set forth the true Christian faith beyond all doubt, the council made that creed which is read in the Communion-service in our churches.[1]

Again, note the fact that this creed was used as a regular part of Christian worship. This is not information for pastors, theologians, or specialists; this is essential truth with which believers need to be inundated regularly—truth I wish I knew when I was a new believer.

> We believe in one God, the Father Almighty;
> Maker of heaven and earth, and of all things visible and invisible.
>
> And in one Lord, Jesus Christ, the only begotten Son of God,
> Begotten of the Father before all worlds,
> God of God, Light of Light,
> Very God of very God,
> Begotten, not made, being of one substance with the Father;
> By whom all things were made;
> Who, for us men and for our salvation
> Came down from heaven,
> And was incarnate by the Holy Ghost of the Virgin Mary,
> And was made man;

And was crucified also for us under Pontius Pilate;
He suffered and was buried;
And the third day he rose again according to the Scriptures;
And ascended into heaven, and sitteth on the right hand of the
     Father;
And he shall come again, with glory, to judge both the quick and
     the dead;
Whose kingdom shall have no end.

And we believe in the Holy Ghost, the Lord and giver of life;
Who proceedeth from the Father and the Son;
Who with the Father and the Son together is worshiped and
     glorified;
Who spake by the prophets.
And we believe in one holy catholic and apostolic church.
We acknowledge one baptism for the remission of sins;
And we look for the resurrection of the dead,
and the life of the world to come. Amen.

As a new believer, I encountered the Jehovah's Witnesses and Mormons with regularity. Unfortunately, I had no Christian background and was not part of a creedal/confessional church. I was ignorant. I had a Bible, but so did they. They also knew their Bibles much better than I knew mine at the time. Doctrine was new and somewhat foreign to me. I knew there were essential truths, but I wasn't sure what those truths were or where to find them. The result was a number of very awkward encounters filled with frustration and confusion.

Then I encountered the Nicene Creed. And in doing so, I discovered that (1) I wasn't dealing with anything new, because (2) this creed addresses the Jehovah's Witness and Mormon heresies directly. Note the statement in the beginning of the main body of the creed:

And in one Lord, Jesus Christ, the only begotten Son of God,
Begotten of the Father before all worlds,
God of God, Light of Light,
Very God of very God,
Begotten, not made, being of one substance with the Father;
By whom all things were made.

I am not suggesting that merely quoting this section of the creed will bring a Jehovah's Witness or a Mormon to his or her knees. On the contrary, most merely shrug creeds off as "man-made," and therefore not trustworthy. However, remember, our goal is not to find words that will have such an effect; there are no words that will do that. Only the Holy Spirit has that kind of power. Our goal is to give an answer for the hope that is in us, and this creed is useful to that end.

Nor is the usefulness of the creed limited to apologetic encounters. These are not truths Christians know intuitively; these are truths we must be taught. The doctrine of the Trinity is as neglected as it is essential. Few Christians have confidence in their grasp of or ability to explain this essential truth. And we must remember that the first step in effective apologetics is knowing what we believe. Thus, these creeds are essential tools for discipleship.

A believer familiar with this creed would not necessarily have to know what the Jehovah's Witnesses or Mormons believe in order to (1) identify their doctrine as different from that which the creed expresses, and, since the creed is an expression of biblical truth, we can (2) know that the Jehovah's Witness and Mormon doctrines are heretical.

The Athanasian Creed

Several years ago, I was invited to participate in an event called The Elephant Room. This event was dedicated to inviting Christian brothers from a broad spectrum of beliefs to sit down and discuss their differences openly and honestly. Unfortunately, the year I was invited was a year filled with controversy. The hosts, James MacDonald and Mark Driscoll, had invited T. D. Jakes to be one of the participants in the event. By the time I got the call, Mark Dever, another Reformed Baptist, had already declined. And, in the end, so did I.

So what was the problem? Put simply, Jakes does not hold to orthodox Christian doctrine in regard to the Trinity (not to mention his commitment to the Word of Faith/Prosperity Gospel, which is no gospel at all). In fact, I had written about Jakes's heretical view almost a decade earlier in my first writing project, *The Ever Loving Truth*.[2] In that eight-week Bible study, I addressed Jakes by name and pointed out his heretical view. So did others, like Hank Hanegraaff, who wrote a cover article on Jakes in his apologetics magazine. This was far from being new to me or to the apologetics community.

The organizers were convinced that Jakes would set the record straight and earn his orthodox *bona fides*. Unfortunately, that did not happen. Anyone familiar with the heresy to which he holds heard him use the familiar and evasive catchphrases and equivocations common in such discussions. He discussed modes and manifestations, and bemoaned the attempts of Christians to be so specific and clear about a doctrine so shrouded in mystery. It was clear to me that there was a way to settle the issue once and for all. There is an ancient creed that was written in response to the very heresy to which Jakes holds (modalism/Sabellianism). We call this the Athanasian Creed (late fifth century).

In a subsequent interview I did with my apologetics hero, James White, he suggested that the only way to deal with Jakes appropriately would have been to nail him down on the categories laid out by the creed:

1. Whosoever will be saved, before all things it is necessary that he hold the Catholic faith. [Though the capitalization of the word *Catholic* usually denotes the Church of Rome, that is not the case here.]
2. Which faith except every one do keep whole and undefiled; without doubt he shall perish everlastingly.
3. And the Catholic faith is this: That we worship one God in Trinity, and Trinity in Unity;
4. Neither confounding the Persons: nor dividing the Substance.
5. For there is one Person of the Father; another of the Son; and another of the Holy Spirit.
6. But the Godhead of the Father, of the Son, and of the Holy Spirit, is all one: the Glory equal, the Majesty coeternal.
7. Such as the Father is; such is the Son; and such is the Holy Spirit.
8. The Father uncreated; the Son uncreated; and the Holy Spirit uncreated.
9. The Father incomprehensible; the Son incomprehensible; and the Holy Spirit incomprehensible.

10. The Father eternal; the Son eternal; and the Holy Spirit eternal.

11. And yet they are not three eternals but one eternal.

12. As also not three uncreated, nor three incomprehensibles, but one uncreated; and one incomprehensible.

13. So likewise the Father is Almighty; the Son Almighty; and the Holy Spirit Almighty.

14. And yet they are not three Almighties but one Almighty.

15. So the Father is God; the Son is God; and the Holy Spirit is God.

16. And yet they are not three Gods but one God.

17. So likewise the Father is Lord; the Son Lord; and the Holy Spirit Lord.

18. And yet not three Lords but one Lord.

19. For like as we are compelled by the Christian verity; to acknowledge every Person by himself to be God and Lord:

20. So are we forbidden by the Catholic Religion to say, There be three Gods, or three Lords.

21. The Father is made of none, neither created nor begotten.

22. The Son is of the Father alone; not made, nor created but begotten.

23. The Holy Spirit is of the Father and of the Son; neither made, nor created, nor begotten, but proceeding.

24. So there is one Father, not three Fathers; one Son, not three Sons; one Holy Spirit, not three Holy Spirits.

25. And in this Trinity none is before or after another; none is greater or less than another.

26. But the whole three Persons are coeternal, and coequal.

27. So that in all things, as aforesaid; the Unity in Trinity, and the Trinity in Unity, is to be worshiped.

28. He therefore that will be saved, must thus think of the Trinity.

29. Furthermore it is necessary to eternal salvation; that he also believe faithfully the incarnation of our Lord Jesus Christ.

30. For the right faith is, that we believe and confess, that our Lord Jesus Christ, the Son of God, is God and Man;

31. God, of the substance of the Father; begotten before the worlds: and Man, of the substance of his Mother, born in the world.

32. Perfect God; and perfect Man, of a reasonable soul and human flesh subsisting.

33. Equal to the Father, as touching his Godhead; and inferior to the Father as touching his Manhood.

34. Who although he be God and Man; yet he is not two, but one Christ.
35. One; not by conversion of the Godhead into flesh; but by taking of the Manhood into God.
36. One altogether; not by confusion of Substance; but by unity of Person.
37. For as the reasonable soul and flesh is one man; so God and Man is one Christ;
38. Who suffered for our salvation: descended into hell; rose again the third day from the dead.
39. He ascended into heaven, he sitteth at the right hand of the Father God Almighty.
40. From whence he shall come to judge the quick and the dead.
41. At whose coming all men shall rise again with their bodies;
42. And shall give account for their own works.
43. And they that have done good shall go into life everlasting; and they that have done evil, into everlasting fire.
44. This is the Catholic Faith; which except a man believed faithfully, he cannot be saved.

Amazingly, many Christians are satisfied with a mere shrug of the shoulders followed by a sigh and the common refrain, "The Trinity is unexplainable, so there's no use trying." How tragic! We have such a clear creedal history demonstrating the commitment of Christians throughout the ages who believed that the Trinity not only *could* be defined and explained, but that it *must* be! This is the God in whom we believe.

CONFESSIONS OF FAITH: THE APOLOGETIC OF THE REFORMATION

In addition to these ancient creeds, we also have a rich, consistent history of confessions that flowed out of the Protestant Reformation. These confessions, unlike the creeds, separate the rest of the world from Rome and define what it means to be Protestant.

The official beginning of the Protestant Reformation was October 31, 1517. On that day, Martin Luther nailed his Ninety-five Theses to the door of the Wittenberg church. The Augsburg Confession followed shortly thereafter in 1530. And while Luther was fighting the good fight in Germany, the Reformation was spreading throughout Europe. The result was a succession of Reformed confessions. These included the Belgic Confession of Faith (1561); the Thirty-Nine Articles (1563, 1571); the Canons of Dort (1618–1619); the First London Baptist Confession (1644); the Westminster Confession of Faith (1646); and the Second London Baptist Confession (1677/1689).

There were certainly others. However, the above list provides more than enough evidence to make the point. Christians have always been creedal/confessional people. And these creeds and confessions have always served at least three purposes. First, confessions of faith serve to unite believers with their historical roots. This has been important since the time of the New Testament, when Paul wrote, "And what you have heard from me in the presence of many witnesses entrust to faithful men who will be able to teach others also" (2 Tim. 2:2). Paul also admonished Timothy to "follow the pattern of the sound words that you have heard from me, in the faith and love that are in Christ Jesus. By the Holy Spirit who dwells within us, guard the good deposit entrusted to you" (2 Tim. 1:13–14). And again, "But as for you, continue in what you have learned and have firmly believed" (2 Tim. 3:14).

The urgency of passing on this "pattern of sound teaching" did not end with the apostles or the New Testament church. This is the obligation of every Christian generation, and our confessions are an expression of our acceptance of that reality. I find it both ironic and disturbing that Christians want to (1) forsake confessionalism and (2) make disciples. The result of this is a kind of remaking Christianity over and over again. It's a bit like having a commitment to training doctors without relying on what we've learned through years of practicing medicine. Certainly we must not be slaves to tradition. However, it is equally wrong to ignore tradition altogether. It's one thing to try to improve on *Gray's Anatomy*; but trying to write an anatomy textbook without relying on or referring to this influential work would be ridiculous.

Second, confessions served to clarify the distinct beliefs of various groups of Christians. For example, in the foreword to the Second London Baptist Confession, the authors wrote, "For the information, and satisfaction of those, that did not thoroughly understand what our principles were, or had entertained prejudices against our Profession." Did you catch that? There were people who, for whatever reason, misunderstood what seventeenth-century Baptists believed, and the confession was designed, at least in part, to confront and correct those misconceptions. In other words, the confession was an apologetic!

Third, confessions serve as a standard and starting point for disciple making. As a father to nine children, I confess that the idea of bringing them up in the discipline and instruction of the Lord (Eph. 6:4) is overwhelming. The same is true for me as a pastor. I can't imagine having to figure out where to start and what to teach.

Again, the foreword to the 1689 Second London Baptist Confession is helpful:

> And verily there is one spring and cause of the decay of Religion in our day, which we cannot but touch upon, and earnestly urge a redress of; and that is the neglect of the worship of God in Families, by those to whom the charge and conduct of them is committed. May not the gross ignorance, and instability of many; with the profaneness of others, be justly charged upon their Parents and Masters; who have not trained them up in the way wherein they ought to walk when they were young? but have neglected those frequent and solemn commands which the Lord hath laid upon them so to catechize, and instruct them, that their tender years might be seasoned with the knowledge of the truth of God as revealed in the Scriptures.

Note that this is the foreword to a thirty-two-chapter minisystematic theology! The idea here is clear: We ought to use our confessions in the discipleship of our children as well as recent converts. This is a hallmark of the Reformed tradition, and we would do well to revive it.

Nor were confessions meant to be substitutes for the Scriptures. C. H. Spurgeon, in his later introduction to the 1689, writes:

> This ancient document is the most excellent epitome of the things most surely believed among us. It is not issued as an authoritative rule or code of faith, whereby you may be fettered, but as a means of edification in righteousness. It is an excellent, though not inspired, expression of the teaching of those Holy Scriptures by which all confessions are to be measured.[3]

In other words, the confession is simply an extended answer to the question, "What do you mean when you say you believe the Bible?" Simply saying, "We believe the Bible," is not enough to distinguish us from the cults, or the Roman Catholics, for that matter. What do we mean by *Bible*? Describing the Bible as the sixty-six books of the Old and New Testaments is a confessional statement. What do we mean by *Jesus*? Defining our christology in a way that differentiates us from the Jehovah's Witnesses, Mormons, Muslims, or Jews is to make a confessional statement. Such distinctions are warranted and necessary.

So what, exactly, do confessions cover? Essentially, they are minisystematic theologies that address the essentials of the faith. For example, here is an outline of the 1689:

The Holy Scriptures
God and the Holy Trinity
God's Decree
Creation
Divine Providence
The Fall of Man, Sin, and Punishment
God's Covenant
Christ the Mediator
Free Will
Effectual Calling
Justification
Adoption
Sanctification
Saving Faith
Repentance and Salvation
Good Works
The Perseverance of the Saints
Assurance of Salvation
The Law of God
The Gospel and Its Influence
Christian Liberty and Liberty of Conscience
Worship and the Sabbath Day
Lawful Oaths and Vows
The Civil Magistrate
Marriage

The Church

The Communion of Saints

Baptism and the Lord's Supper

Baptism

The Lord's Supper

Man's State after Death and the Resurrection

The Last Judgment

These thirty-two chapters express beliefs held among Baptists since the Reformation. *That* is a useful document! Of course, there is not room enough to discuss the confession in its entirety. However, in order to demonstrate its usefulness, allow me to share two paragraphs.

The paragraph to which I refer more often than any other in the Second London Baptist Confession is paragraph 1 of chapter 3: "God's Decree":

> God hath decreed in himself from all eternity, by the most wise and holy counsel of his own will, freely and unchangeably, all things whatsoever comes to pass; yet so as thereby is God neither the author of sin, nor hath fellowship with any therein, nor is violence offered to the will of the creature, nor yet is the liberty, or contingency of second causes taken away, but rather established, in which appears his wisdom in disposing all things, and power, and faithfulness in accomplishing his decree.

The richness of this one paragraph and its usefulness in apologetics has become as dear to me in recent days as any other single tool. I refer to this paragraph in sermons, personal encounters, and private devotions, as it is one of the clearest and most concise expressions you will find concerning a truth that confounds both Christians and non-Christians alike. I have referred to this paragraph (and the rest of the paragraphs in this chapter) in answering questions like, "How does God know everything?" or, "Why does God allow evil?" and, "If God uses the actions of evil men, then doesn't that make him the author of evil?" It has also been helpful in answering the age-old question, "If God knows everything, then why do my actions and choices matter?"

Again, this statement in the confession in and of itself is not the answer to all our problems. It is merely a tool. However, it is a useful and powerful tool in the sense that it clarifies and codifies biblical truth in a concise and helpful manner. This is also true of my favorite paragraph in chapter 8, "Christ the Mediator":

> The Son of God, the second person in the Holy Trinity, being very and eternal God, the brightness of the Father's glory, of one substance and equal with him: who made the World, who upholdeth and governeth all things he hath made, did when the fullness of time was come take unto him man's nature, with all the essential properties, and common infirmities thereof, yet without sin, being conceived by the Holy Spirit in the womb of the Virgin Mary, the Holy Spirit coming down upon her, and the power of the most High overshadowing her, and so was made of a woman, of the tribe of Judah, of the seed of Abraham, and David according to the Scriptures; So that two whole, perfect, and distinct natures, were inseparably joined together in one person: without conversion, composition, or confusion; which person is very God, and very Man; yet one Christ, the only Mediator between God and Man.

This paragraph is a favorite of mine for at least two reasons. First, it magnifies Christ! The language here elicits honor, reverence, and worship. Who Christ is and what he has done is beyond comprehension. Yet, God has revealed the truth of Christ's person and work in his Word. What an incredible blessing!

Second, this paragraph is a clear reflection of the ancient creeds. It is connected to the rich biblical, theological history of the people of God, and thus creates a sense of synergy for the disciple seeking to understand the majesty of Christ. And, more to our point, it serves as another layer of preparation for expository apologetics. The question, then, is, "How do we put it all together?"

CATECHISM: THE FOUNDATION AND GLUE

"Daddy, why did Jesus have to die?" For three straight days, that was the question one of my children asked during family worship. We were working our way through the book of Hebrews and learning a great deal about Christ's sacrificial death and its implications. Each night I went back over the texts we had been studying and explained the gospel. It was a precious time. However, on the third day, when the question came, I had decided to do something different. I knew my son was asking the question because he was just not quite ready to comprehend the truths to which he was being exposed. Nevertheless, I wanted him to know that he already knew the answer to his question. So, instead of my usual response, I just asked a series of questions—questions I had asked him and his siblings literally hundreds of times. I asked the following questions, and they gave the following responses:

Q. What is a covenant?
A. A covenant is an agreement between two or more persons.

Q. What is the covenant of grace?
A. It is an eternal agreement within the Trinity to save certain persons called the elect, and to provide all the means for their salvation.

Q. What did Christ undertake in the covenant of grace?
A. Christ undertook to keep the whole law for his people, and to suffer the punishment due to their sins.

Q. Did our Lord Jesus Christ ever sin?
A. No. He was holy, blameless, and undefiled.

Q. How could the Son of God suffer?
A. Christ, the Son of God, took flesh and blood, that he might obey and suffer as a man.

Q. What is meant by the atonement?
A. The atonement consists of Christ's satisfying divine justice, by his sufferings and death, in the place of sinners.

Q. For whom did Christ obey and suffer?
A. Christ obeyed and suffered for those whom the Father had given him.

Q. What kind of life did Christ live on earth?
A. Christ lived a life of perfect obedience to the law of God.

Q. What kind of death did Christ die?
A. Christ experienced the painful and shameful death of the cross.

Q. Who will be saved?
A. Only those who repent of sin and believe in Christ will be saved.

Q. What is it to repent?
A. Repentance involves sorrow for sin, leading one to hate and forsake it because it is displeasing to God.

Q. What is it to believe in Christ?
A. A person believes who knows that his only hope is Christ and trusts in Christ alone for salvation.

Oh, to have the literary skill of Dickens, Updike, or Hawthorne to describe the look on my child's face the moment he realized not only that there was an answer to his question, but that he knew it all along! As a father, it was better than giving the proverbial "perfect gift" and getting quintessential response. My child did not come to faith in Christ that day. However, he came to realize that the rote memorization he was doing each morning actually had purpose. More importantly, he realized that it was providing him with real answers to his very real questions about God's Word.

Little did my son, or the rest of my children, know that they were being equipped for expository apologetics. They were learning what to believe, why to believe it, and how to communicate it in a clear, winsome manner. Apologetics is about giving answers to people's legitimate questions about what we believe. Catechism is learning what we believe by memorizing answers to questions. Perfect! Yet, again, how many times have we thought to ourselves, "Apologetics is for specialists, philosophers, and extraordinary debaters"?

PUTTING IT ALL TOGETHER

If we understand apologetics as vindication of the Christian world and life view against all others, and approach that task through the framework of Peter's admonition to know what we believe and why we believe it, and to always be prepared to communicate that to others in an effective, winsome manner (see 1 Pet. 3:15), then creeds, confessions, and catechisms become more than mere historical novelties. These are actually the essential tools of our trade.

First, these tools are effective. They prepare us to do the work of apologetics. These tools take the guesswork out of the apologetic task. No longer are we tossed to and fro trying to figure out what everyone else believes, or how we can convince them of God's existence without using the Bible. We simply commit ourselves to pursuing a deep, abiding knowledge and understanding of our own faith.

Second, these tools are portable. We can leave them with our interlocutors. When we find ourselves engaged in an expository apologetic encounter where the truths of these creeds, confessions, and catechisms form the basis for our defense, we can very easily point them to the source. And, since these tools include Scripture references, we are pointing people ultimately to the Word of God.

Third, these tools are transferrable. We can use them to disciple young Christians and raise our children in historic, thoughtful, systematic ways that will help them know what they believe and why they believe it, and to be able to communicate their belief effectively and winsomely to others.

My hope in this chapter is that you will see the relevance and importance of creeds, confessions, and catechisms. Also, I hope you are continuing to change the way you view apologetics. As I've said, I believe the idea of apologetics as a philosophical discipline reserved for specialists is (1) unbiblical and (2) harmful. As we saw in chapter 2, the New Testament presents apologetics as a discipline for every believer. As such, preparation for apologetics must include every Christian. In this chapter, we have seen how using creeds, catechisms, and confessions achieves both ends.

In the next chapter, we will look at a specific application of this idea. Catechisms generally concentrate on four basic areas. First, they teach biblical truth about creation and the fall. Second, they teach basic biblical truth about salvation/redemption. Third, they teach the basics of prayer through the Lord's Prayer. Fourth, they teach basic Christian ethics from the foundation of the Ten Commandments. In chapter 6, we will examine the application of this fourth emphasis of catechesis to expository apologetics. How do we address contemporary moral issues from a biblical perspective? How do we answer the objections of those who believe doing so is outdated, or even immoral? Let us turn our attention to these questions.

6

The Ten Commandments

So far we have established that the law is relevant to expository apologetics. We have also answered the objection posed by those who believe it is hypocritical to apply some parts of the law and not others. Additionally, we have established the fact that those who disagree with us are actually the ones who arbitrarily pick and choose. They hold to certain parts of the law and not to others. In fact, their objection to our use of the law is based on their assumption that hypocrisy is wrong—an idea rooted in the ninth commandment. The difference, of course, is that (1) we know we are using the law, and they do not; (2) we know why we are picking and choosing, and they do not; and (3) our picking and choosing is governed by an authority outside ourselves, and theirs is not.

Now we must determine the best way to use the law in an expository apologetic encounter. As we do, we must keep three things in mind. First, whatever we do must be rooted in the power, simplicity, and authority of Scripture. We have to use the Bible in a way that demonstrates our dependence on an outside authority as we contrast that with man's desire to serve as his own judge and authority. Using the law is the ultimate example of this principle.

Second, our use of the law must be easy to remember. The key to expository apologetics is being able to engage in normal, everyday conversations. Toward that end, we will work on memorizing the Ten Commandments in this chapter. This is not only very doable—children have been doing it throughout the history of the church—it is also very helpful, because the Decalogue is foundational to so much of what we do and think.

Third, everything we do must be conversational. And by conversational, I mean it must be natural, reasonable, and winsome. Remember, our goal is to engage in discussion, not debate. We are helping people see the holes in their reasoning while at the same time demonstrating the coherence in our own. We are not scolding people who are inferior to us; we are helping people who are standing exactly where we once stood. These are people made in the image of God—people who matter to him and ought to matter to us.

With that in mind, let us examine the Decalogue. We will begin by listing the Ten Commandments. Then we will look at four of them through the hermeneutical lens of the Sermon on the Mount. Finally, we will explore the work of one of, if not the greatest, assembly of theologians in church history, the Westminster Larger Catechism. Our aim is to apply the law to practical Christian ethics while keeping in mind the goal of expository apologetics and the audience to whom we are trying to communicate.

THE TEN COMMANDMENTS

Most Christians I meet today are unfamiliar with the Ten Commandments. Hence, we must begin at the beginning:

1. Have no other gods.
2. Have no idols.
3. Do not profane the Lord's name.
4. Remember the Sabbath.
5. Honor your father and mother.
6. Do not murder.
7. Do not commit adultery.
8. Do not steal.
9. Do not bear false witness.
10. Do not covet.

Anyone desiring to be an effective expository apologist would do well to memorize that list. But before we move on, here are a few observations.

First, the Ten Commandments are divided into two parts, or two "tables" of the law. The first four are vertical. The last six are horizontal. That is, the first four emphasize our duty to God. The last six emphasize our duty to other people.

Second, each table of the law is summed up in a single command. Jesus summarizes the first in this way: "You shall love the Lord your God with all your heart and with all your soul and with all your mind. This is the great and first commandment" (Matt. 22:37–38, cf. Deut. 6:5). He then adds, "And a second is like it: You shall love your neighbor as yourself" (Matt. 22:39, cf. Lev. 19:18).

Third, these summaries, far from nullifying the law, serve to highlight its importance in the Christian life. For example, the apostle Paul writes:

> Owe no one anything, except to love each other, for the one who loves another has fulfilled the law. For the commandments, "You shall not commit adultery, You shall not murder, You shall not steal, You shall not covet," and any other commandment, are summed up in this word: "You shall love your neighbor as yourself." Love does no wrong to a neighbor; therefore love is the fulfilling of the law. (Rom. 13:8–10)

Note that Paul makes reference to adultery (seventh commandment), murder (sixth commandment), theft (eighth commandment), and coveting (tenth commandment) in relation to his call to a love that "does no wrong to a neighbor." This is not a call to sentimentality; it is a call to righteousness as defined by the second table of the law.

It may seem a bit awkward at first, but I assure you that becoming fluent in the Ten Commandments is a worthy goal. As we will see, fluency in the law will be of great benefit (1) to your own soul as it shapes your ethics, (2) to your efforts in expository apologetics as you challenge the ethics of others, and (3) in your effort to engage little ones and/or new converts as you take on the Great Commission task of "teaching them to observe all that I have commanded you" (Matt. 28:20).

The Ten Commandments and the Sermon on the Mount

The Sermon on the Mount is the fountainhead of Christian ethics. It is also the hermeneutical key that unlocks the law for the believer. Here

Jesus makes it clear that (1) the law is both good and permanent, (2) we are incapable of keeping it in and of ourselves, and (3) we as Christians are both able and expected to go beyond it because of our union and communion with Christ. Two examples of Jesus's use of the law provide great insight:

> You have heard that it was said to those of old, "You shall not murder; and whoever murders will be liable to judgment." But I say to you that everyone who is angry with his brother will be liable to judgment; whoever insults his brother will be liable to the council; and whoever says, "You fool!" will be liable to the hell of fire. (Matt. 5:21–22)

The first thing of note is the common refrain, "You have heard that it was said. . . . But I say to you . . ." (cf. Matt 5:21, 27, 33, 38, 43). Robert Mounce, commenting on this pattern, notes that "Jesus does not contradict what was said but brings it into sharper ethical focus."[1] In other words, Jesus is not saying that the law given to and through Moses was inferior. Instead, he is saying that it meant, and means, much more than anyone, including Moses, ever thought or was able to think. Now Jesus, the incarnate Word, reveals just how holy God is, and how much his holiness requires.

This is an important and powerful tool for the expository apologist. First, this passage elevates one of the laws upon which we can all agree, the sixth commandment. Second, it does so in a way that shows Jesus's commitment to the law. He is not here writing a new law; he is showing solidarity with the existing law. Third, it does so in a way that exposes the heart of every sinner. Every person has been guilty of this kind of hatred at one time or another. Finally, it does so in a way that shows great disdain for religious hypocrisy.

All of these things pull our interlocutors onto our platform. They want brotherly kindness. To quote Jack Black's character in *Proposition 8: The Musical*, "Please choose love instead of hate." Well, this takes love vs. hate out of the philosophical realm and puts feet on it! Moreover, remember that Black's character was none other than Jesus. The idea touted by the "you pick and choose" crowd is that Jesus is the prophet of love and Christians are not being like him. This example from the Sermon on the Mount shows that we are being like him.

This example, and the ones that follow, serve to guide us in our thinking about the Decalogue. We see here that the commandments have greater depth and breadth; they encompass the spirit as well as the letter of the law. This gives us an even broader scope in terms of Christian ethics (as we will see later).

The second example is important in that it gets to the heart of the seventh commandment and the most critical moral issues of Jesus's day—and ours:

> You have heard that it was said, "You shall not commit adultery." But I say to you that everyone who looks at a woman with lustful intent has already committed adultery with her in his heart. (Matt. 5:27–28)

This passage may not seem like much. However, it is an expository apologetic goldmine! (1) These verses bring the seventh commandment to bear on every aspect of human sexuality. (2) They combat the notion that sexuality is fluid. Jesus addresses men and women with no room for other alternatives. (3) They demolish the idea that "love" is the fountainhead of sexual ethics. There is no room for the "the heart wants what it wants" school of sexual mores. (4) They place guilt in the heart/mind, thus calling into account even those who, like monks and priests, practice outward celibacy for holiness.

Rosaria Butterfield is a former professor at Syracuse University. In her book, *Secret Thoughts of an Unlikely Convert,* she recounts her journey from anti-Christian lesbianism to Reformed Christianity. In addressing her prior sexuality, she puts her finger squarely on the matter: "Sexuality isn't about what we do in bed. Sexuality encompasses a whole range of needs, demands, and desires. Sexuality is more a symptom of our life's condition than a cause, more a consequence than an origin."[2] Then, with the keen insight and brutal honesty that characterizes the book, she diagnoses her past sexual encounters in a manner consistent with Jesus's assessment:

> My moral code encompassed serial monogamy, "safe" sex, and sex only in the context of love. Love, grounded only in personal feelings

as mine had been, changes without warning or logic. The truth is, outside of Christ, I am a manipulator, liar, power-monger, and controller. In my relationships with men and with women, I had to be in charge. I killed with kindness and slayed with gifts. I bought people's loyalties and affections.[3]

This is what every sinner needs to see about his or her sexuality. It's not about what you do or with whom as much as it is about who you are and what motivates your actions. Sexual sin does not start in the bedroom; it starts in the mind . . . and in the heart. This is what Jesus is saying, and this is what the expository apologist needs to communicate.

Jesus elevates our understanding of the law and points his hearers in at least two directions. First, and most obviously, he addresses those who do not attempt to keep the law. This is his irreligious audience. To them, Jesus affirms and confirms God's law and the penalties attached thereto. He makes it clear, as Paul does later, "that the unrighteous will not inherit the kingdom of God" (1 Cor. 6:9).

Second, and more importantly, Jesus addresses those who think they keep the law by mere outward conformity. This is his religious audience. Here, Jesus makes it clear that the religious person offering mere outward adherence to the law falls just as short as the irreligious person who ignores it. As Calvin notes:

> Our Lord explains more fully, by minute instances, by what tortuous methods the Pharisees debase the law, so that their righteousness is mere filth. It is a mistake, however, to suppose that this is an ἐπανόρθωσις, or correction of the Law, and that Christ raises his disciples to a higher degree of perfection, than Christ could raise a gross and carnal nation, which was scarcely able to learn first principles.[4]

This is the most shocking aspect of the Sermon on the Mount. It is also the most useful to the expository apologist.

It is a powerful thing to look a person in the eye and say, "I'm not a murderer, but I am guilty of the hatred at the very root of murder, and am, therefore, guilty before a holy God, and I need a Savior who is as pure inside as he is outside." This is a powerful way to get to the gospel! It dispels the myth of Christian self-righteousness. It exposes the self-righteousness in our interlocutors who, whether they admit it or not, believe themselves to be righteous; in fact, they believe themselves to be more righteous than we are because we are hypocrites who "pick and choose" what laws we will uphold. And it juxtaposes God's holiness and man's sinfulness in a way that magnifies Christ, which is our ultimate goal.

THE TEN COMMANDMENTS AND EXPOSITORY APOLOGETICS

I will never forget the first time I heard someone teach Christian ethics from the Decalogue. The teacher was John Frame from Reformed Theological Seminary. I found his lectures on iTunes and began to listen to them on my morning walks. I was blown away! I did not grow up in a Christian home. In fact, I didn't hear the gospel and come to faith until I was in college. I was not introduced to Reformed theology until after graduating from seminary. Up to that point, I had been educated in an environment of vaguely Arminian, vaguely dispensational, pragmatic-utilitarian, anti-Calvinistic, quasifundamentalism. My journey to Reformed theology took place mainly in the form of reading new books by men like John Piper, D. A. Carson, Alistair Begg, and others, who kept referring to dusty old books. It was in the dusty old books that I discovered the roots of this robust, intensely theological, Christ-exalting, soul-stirring . . . stuff.

Then I discovered RTS online. I began to go back through courses that I had already taken and passed, but had not understood from a Reformed context. It was like learning to walk again; it was glorious, exhilarating, and painful all at the same time. Then I discovered Frame's lectures on Christian ethics, and pieces began to fall into place. Suddenly, I saw what had been missing: confessionalism and the law. Sure, in my journey to Reformed doctrine, I had discovered both. I was a committed Reformed Baptist, holding to the Second London Baptist Confession of 1689, and I had abandoned dispensationalism and its view of the law. However, I had not made the connection between those two things and the formation of Christian ethics. I drank in Frame's lectures like a thirsty man trying to drink from a fire hydrant; the more

I drank, the thirstier I got, and the thirstier I got, the more there was to drink.

In his lectures, Frame did not legalistically attempt to use the law and confession as a wooden standard. Instead, he reached into the rich heritage and tradition of the Reformed faith to (1) demonstrate the relevance of the Decalogue to Christian ethics, (2) show how our forefathers had handled these issues and what we can learn from them, and (3) provide a framework for ongoing understanding and application in personal life and pastoral ministry. And as an expository apologist, I found it refreshing, encouraging, and quite appropriate that Frame also taught apologetics.[5]

MAKING THE CONNECTION

How, then, do we employ the Ten Commandments in our execution of expository apologetics? How do we go from knowing the Ten Commandments and understanding how to interpret them in light of the New Covenant to applying them in conversations with people who are not only ignorant of them, but also likely to be antagonistic?

First, remember, our goal is not to convince people to follow the Ten Commandments. We simply want to show them that (1) the ethical issues about which they are concerned matter to God; (2) because these issues matter to God, they also matter to us; and (3) God has given us a standard by which we may judge these issues—a standard that is outside of and superior to ourselves.

Second, remember that this is not a match of wits, but a spiritual encounter. We must rely on the Word that "is living and active, sharper than any two-edged sword, piercing to the division of soul and of spirit, of joints and of marrow, and discerning the thoughts and intentions of the heart" (Heb. 4:12). Training our minds to evaluate ethical issues through the lens of the Decalogue is not as complicated as it seems.

For the sake of space, I will limit this discussion to the first four commandments. Also, since the nature of the second table of the law is in keeping with the discussion in the previous chapter, it seems fitting to leave that for now. Also while the second table of the law elicits scorn from atheists, the first table makes even born-again Christians howl! Many believe that there is no room in a civilized society for people who insist on making the first four commandments a matter of public morality.

With that in mind, I will attempt the following: (1) I will quote the commandment as it is written in Exodus 20; (2) I will provide the Westminster Larger Catechism commentary on the commandment; (3) I will offer a few examples of contemporary issues we may address using the specific commandment; and (4) I will give examples of encounters.

The First Commandment: No Other Gods

As Israel came out of Egypt, there were a number of pieces of spiritual baggage they needed to unload. Chief among them was polytheism. In Egypt, they had been exposed to the idea that there were many gods, including Pharaoh himself. However, Yahweh wanted to make it clear that there is only one God, and it is he:

> You shall have no other gods before me. (Ex. 20:3)

The Westminster divines offered the following catechesis to explain and expand the first commandment:

> Q. 46. What is required in the first commandment?
> A. The first commandment requireth us to know and acknowledge God to be the only true God, and our God; and to worship and glorify him accordingly.

> Q. 47. What is forbidden in the first commandment?
> A. The first commandment forbiddeth the denying, or not worshiping and glorifying the true God as God, and our God; and the giving of that worship and glory to any other which is due to him alone.[6]

The first commandment is central to issues like religious freedom, separation of church and state, government education, and the Christian's role in the political arena, to name a few. I have come to realize the importance of the first commandment as I have engaged in discussions about the hot-button issues of the day. In doing so, I have noticed several things that have brought me back again and again to my belief that the first commandment is foundational to the modern secularist debate.

One thing that keeps me running back to this commandment is the existence of moral absolutes. A culture that holds to moral absolutes while denying the existence of God or failing to acknowledge and acquiesce to God, is a culture on a rapid, one-way course to moral decay and nihilism. And that is precisely what we face today. Allow me to illustrate.

Our culture continues to cling to a number of moral absolutes. (1) We believe that slavery was a great injustice, and must never be tolerated. (2) We believe that discrimination is abhorrent, and must be eliminated. (3) We believe it is wrong to abuse children. There are exceptions to every one of these. However, those exceptions are in the minority. For the most part, these are ideas held universally among Americans.

Ironically, another idea held almost universally among Americans is that you can't force your beliefs on others. The irony, of course, is that none of us object to forcing our beliefs about slavery, discrimination, or child abuse on others. The result is a cognitive dissonance that goes unaddressed. Even Christians search feverishly for answers to modern ethical dilemmas that do not rely on biblical truth. God forbid we should press the antithesis and bring the first commandment to bear.

Another thing that keeps me running back to the first commandment is American history. The first time I visited Washington, DC, and the surrounding areas, I was struck by the beauty and grandeur of it all. I was also struck by the unabashed biblical references that were ubiquitous. Similarly, as I began reading to my children, I discovered things about our nation's history that made me scratch my head in amazement; I also became angry as I realized how duped I had been!

I had come to believe that America was a secular state, a land where people had come to escape religious tyranny; in doing so, they had left behind their "Old World" superstitions. What I discovered, though, was something quite different. I discovered a biblical, theological foundation that served to underscore and explain *everything*. For example, I found statements like article 19 of the New Jersey Constitution of 1776:

> That there shall be no establishment of any one religious sect in this Province, in preference to another; and that no Protestant inhabitant of this Colony shall be denied the enjoyment of any civil right, merely on account of his religious principles; but that all persons,

professing a belief in the faith of any Protestant sect, who shall demean themselves peaceably under the government, as hereby established, shall be capable of being elected into any office of profit or trust, or being a member of either branch of the Legislature, and shall fully and freely enjoy every privilege and immunity, enjoyed by others their fellow subjects.

But, wait! Haven't we always been told that the American ideal was a secular state where *everyone's religion is treated equally?*

It is hard to believe that not so long ago, the Pennsylvania Constitution (1776) required that "each member [of the house of representatives], before he takes his seat, shall make and subscribe the following declaration, viz":

I do believe in one God, the creator and governor of the universe, the rewarder of the good and the punisher of the wicked. And I do acknowledge the Scriptures of the Old and New Testament to be given by Divine inspiration.

It is almost impossible to imagine such a thing today. In fact, if you were educated in government schools in the past half century, you've probably never heard such a thing! You may even be tempted to believe I just made it up. And if that is the case, you certainly won't believe what was written in the Constitution of South Carolina:

That all persons and religious societies who acknowledge that there is one God, and a future state of rewards and punishments, and that God is publicly to be worshipped, shall be freely tolerated. The Christian Protestant religion shall be deemed, and is hereby constituted and declared to be, the established religion of this State. That all denominations of Christian Protestants in this State, demeaning themselves peaceably and faithfully, shall enjoy equal religious and civil privileges. (Article 38, 1787)

Nine years after the South Carolina Constitution was written, George Washington would repeat this sentiment in his farewell address:

The name of American, which belongs to you in your national capacity, must always exalt the just pride of patriotism more than any appellation derived from local discriminations. With slight shades of difference, you have the same religion, manners, habits, and political principles.[7]

Today, Muslims want to build a mosque in the shadow of what many see as their great conquest of 9/11, and those who oppose it are chided because of their hypocritical intolerance. "How dare you stand here in the land of 'Religious Freedom' and deny that freedom to anyone!" Of course, my point here is not that all Muslims, Hindus, or Buddhists should be run out of the country. I do not believe that. I am simply saying that the change in religious landscape means a change in foundational assumptions about ethics and morality. And this change wreaks havoc on the moral fabric of a society.

I am saying that today's lawmakers cannot make good and just laws to undergird, and/or expand upon prior laws, unless those laws are rooted in the same truth that shaped their predecessors. I am saying that judges cannot interpret laws rightly in the American context without understanding that the foundation of those laws, historically, was based in biblical truth. I am saying that citizens cannot govern themselves, nor can the police keep the peace unless we hold to some kind of shared morality based on something other than prevailing sentiment.

Nor is this idea original to me. Much greater minds than mine have made this exact same argument:

> Of all the dispositions and habits which lead to political prosperity, religion and morality are indispensable supports. In vain would that man claim the tribute of patriotism, who should labor to subvert these great pillars of human happiness, these firmest props of the duties of men and citizens. The mere politician, equally with the pious man, ought to respect and to cherish them. A volume could not trace all their connections with private and public felicity. Let it simply be asked: Where is the security for property, for reputation, for life, if the sense of religious obligation desert the oaths which are the instruments of investigation in courts of justice? And let us with caution indulge the supposition that morality can be maintained without religion. Whatever may be conceded to the influence of

refined education on minds of peculiar structure, reason and experience both forbid us to expect that national morality can prevail in exclusion of religious principle.[8]

In case you were wondering, that was our first president, on the occasion of his farewell address. George Washington, like all his contemporaries, knew very well that there could be no meaningful, sustainable morality without religion. Today, politicians, professors, and the populous are all arguing the exact opposite. The result is secular humanism, cognitive dissonance, moral decay, and nihilism.

Nor is the period of our founding the only place one can find such evidence. Ironically, we can also turn to a series of events that corrected a great evil that our founders failed to address. That issue was slavery.

It was an appeal to God and his law that broke the back of slavery in America. It was the same appeal that later broke the back of discrimination during the civil rights era. The leaders of the abolitionist movement, and those who led the charge in the civil rights movement, all appealed to Scripture in their efforts to call America to repent. It was the shared understanding that our rights come from God and that all people are made in God's image that led to change.

Today, people want to uphold, applaud, and identify with the aforementioned movements, while ignoring or even condemning the foundation upon which they were built. Homosexual advocates appeal to the civil rights movement like a ventriloquist hoping you don't see his lips moving. The last thing they want is for people to connect the civil rights movement with its biblical/theological moorings. No one wants to mention the fact that the leaders of the movement were pastors appealing to God's law as the basis for their argument. To acknowledge this would cause the entire argument to crumble like a house of cards.

The expository apologist must not shy away from pressing the first commandment. God will not be ignored. Men owe God worship. To know this and act as though failing to render to God that which is due is somehow unimportant is to do men a terrible disservice. It is also a recipe for eventual judgment.

The Second Commandment: No Idols

If we understand the basis for applying the first commandment to modern American morality, then the second commandment follows logically. If we must acknowledge that there is but one God, then we must also refuse to acknowledge and/or worship other gods.

> You shall not make for yourself a carved image, or any likeness of anything that is in heaven above, or that is in the earth beneath, or that is in the water under the earth. (Ex. 20:4)

The Westminster divines offered the following catechesis to explain and expand the second commandment:

> Q. 50. What is required in the second commandment?
> A. The second commandment requireth the receiving, observing, and keeping pure and entire, all such religious worship and ordinances as God hath appointed in his Word.

> Q. 51. What is forbidden in the second commandment?
> A. The second commandment forbiddeth the worshiping of God by images, or any other way not appointed in his Word.[9]

The second commandment is central to our understanding of issues like public religious observance and religious discrimination. A recent example of this took center stage at Harvard University. On May 12, 2014, CNN reported, "A Harvard club's plans to stage a satanic 'black Mass' were abruptly cancelled Monday after drawing fire from the Archdiocese of Boston and condemnation from the president of the Ivy League school."[10] The decision to cancel this event was important and informative.

It was important because the issue of satanic worship is abhorrent and should be condemned. It was encouraging to see the almost universal rejection of the event proposed by the satanic campus organization. The decision was informative because it exposed the hypocrisy and cognitive dissonance of secularism.

Harvard is a hotbed for liberalism, political correctness, and tolerance. The school embraces postmodern, secular human, nihilistic ethics, and will barely tolerate Bible believers in its divinity school, let alone among the general faculty. So why would they draw the line *anywhere*? Why was the "black mass" a bridge too far? The answer really doesn't matter. What matters is that the Harvard decision proves an important point. Societies have to make decisions about the second commandment.

Unfortunately, our society has been almost as keen to eliminate the worship of Yahweh as Harvard was to eliminate the black mass. Recent court cases brought by groups like Citizens United for the Separation of Church and State have sought to end public expressions of Christian faith such as nativity scenes, crosses, Ten Commandment displays, public prayer, "one nation under God" in the pledge, and the mention of God at graduation ceremonies. No doubt someone will come after the last stanza of our national anthem:

> O thus be it ever, when freemen shall stand
> Between their loved home and the war's desolation!
> Blest with vict'ry and peace, may the heav'n rescued land
> Praise the Power that hath made and preserved us a nation.
> Then conquer we must, when our cause it is just,
> And this be our motto: "In God is our trust."
> And the star-spangled banner in triumph shall wave
> O'er the land of the free and the home of the brave![11]

For the expository apologist, the Harvard decision is a line in the sand that can also serve as a touchstone for conversations about the application of the second commandment to public morality. Again, this matters because it matters to God. The worship of idols is abhorrent. As Paul waited for his travel companions in Athens, Luke records that "his spirit was provoked within him as he saw that the city was full of idols" (Acts 17:16). May we be no less provoked by violations of the second commandment in our day.

The Third Commandment: No Profanity

The third commandment is often overlooked:

> You shall not take the name of the LORD your God in vain, for the LORD will not hold him guiltless who takes his name in vain. (Ex. 20:7)

The Westminster divines offered the following catechesis to explain and expand the third commandment:

Q. 54. What is required in the third commandment?
A. The third commandment requireth the holy and reverent use of God's names, titles, attributes, ordinances, Word, and works.

Q. 55. What is forbidden in the third commandment?
A. The third commandment forbiddeth all profaning or abusing anything whereby God maketh himself known.[12]

The third commandment is central to issues like public decency. And, although we live in a time where the application of this aspect of the moral law seems absurd, there was a time when it was enforced even in Hollywood. The Motion Picture Production Code of 1930, also known as the Hays Code, governed the moral content of motion pictures.[13] Among other things, the code addressed the issues of obscenity and profanity:

Obscenity
Obscenity in word, gesture, reference, song, joke, or by suggestion (even when likely to be understood only by part of the audience) is forbidden.

Profanity
Pointed profanity (this includes the words, God, Lord, Jesus, Christ—unless used reverently—Hell, SOB, damn, Gawd), or every other profane or vulgar expression however used, is forbidden.[14]

Whether the Hays Code was an appropriate application of moral law is debatable. However, what is not debatable is the fact that we see, once again, an attempt to conform public morality to biblical truth. There must always be a standard, and for most of our history, we looked to the Bible to discover what that standard was. Today people not only reject the Bible as a standard; they also view those who would do so as guilty of violating the moral standard of the day! Ironically, imposing religious morals on others is to today's culture what promoting obscenity and profanity was in 1930. We have not given up on the idea of public morality; we've just chosen a different morality.

For example, several years ago there was an art collection that contained a piece called Piss Christ. The photograph was of a crucifix submerged in a container of urine. There was much debate as to whether it was right to ban the piece. Ironically, I was able to use this event a number of times as I argued *against* banning the piece. Of course, I wanted the piece banned. However, my goal was to force unbelievers to make an argument for banning the piece without relying on the third commandment. Then I would ask questions like, "What standard would you use to determine which art to ban?"

In several conversations people had to admit that they (1) relied on the Christian worldview without knowing it, (2) made an argument that would result in an unsustainable precedent, and (3) had no alternative but to support the piece or abandon their non-Christian philosophy of life. (Of course, it wasn't that simple.)

The Fourth Commandment: The Lord's Day

The fourth commandment is rejected almost as much by Christians as it is by non-Christians today. This is tragic on many levels; but for our purposes, the tragedy lies in the fact that we are missing a golden opportunity to press the claims of Yahweh in an antagonistic culture. The fourth commandment reads:

> Remember the Sabbath day, to keep it holy. Six days you shall labor, and do all your work, but the seventh day is a Sabbath to the LORD your God. On it you shall not do any work, you, or your son, or your daughter, your male servant, or your female servant, or your livestock, or the sojourner who is within your gates. For in six days the LORD made heaven and earth, the sea, and all that is in them, and rested on the seventh day. Therefore the LORD blessed the Sabbath day and made it holy. (Ex. 20:8–11)

The Westminster divines offered the following catechesis to explain and expand the fourth commandment:

> Q. 58. What is required in the fourth commandment?
> A. The fourth commandment requireth the keeping holy to God such set times as he appointed in his Word; expressly one whole day in seven to be a holy sabbath to himself.

Q. 61. What is forbidden in the fourth commandment?

A. The fourth commandment forbiddeth the omission or careless performance of the duties required, and the profaning the day by idleness, or doing that which is in itself sinful, or by unnecessary thoughts, words, or works, about our worldly employments or recreations.[15]

Many believe the only application of the fourth commandment is Sabbath observance. However, that is not true. The fourth commandment is central to issues like employment, incarceration, and even the treatment of animals. The fourth commandment is the reason it is wrong to require people—or animals—to work seven days a week. It's amazing that even the concept of a day off has its roots in God's law. Don't believe me? Try making an argument for it from any other authoritative moral source.

A concept that gained traction when I was in high school was the idea of the "sweatshop." A famous shoe company was using factories in China to crank out its one-hundred-dollar high-tops, and when people found out how long workers were working and how little they were being paid, moral outrage erupted. "How could they do such a thing?" "I'll never buy their shoes again!" Of course, if I knew then what I know now (and if I had been a Christian, or had even heard the gospel at that point in my life), I would have viewed it as a golden opportunity to demonstrate the relevance and necessity of the Ten Commandments in general, and the fourth commandment in particular.

People are concerned about the rights and treatment of workers, and rightfully so. God is also concerned about them. However, apart from God, we are hard-pressed to figure out what is moral and what is not. We are hard-pressed to figure out where we should start thinking about an issue, or where that thinking should take us in terms of action. Praise God! We have not been left alone on the matter.

A CRITICAL PIECE OF THE PUZZLE

I believe ignorance of, and open opposition to God's law is the most crucial issue facing our society today. It is more important than abortion, same-sex "marriage," or anything else that may come down the road, because it lays the groundwork for how we think about every issue that comes along. Once we decide that we live in a secular society that demands nonreligious solutions to all our problems, we concede the battlefield, and the end-game is inevitable. Even if we are successful in any area of moral concern, it is a pyrrhic victory at best. Winning a battle while failing to acknowledge God (1) is disobedience to God's command, (2) is a concession to the larger point that a secular society is worth having, and (3) results in temporary laws that will last only as long as public opinion holds.

This is an untenable position for the expository apologist. Our road may be long and the climb steep, but there is no alternative. We must obey God rather than man. And we must acknowledge God. Failure to do so is both sinful and dangerous. If we believe that "Blessed is the nation whose God is the LORD" (Ps. 33:12) and that "Righteousness exalts a nation, but sin is a reproach to any people" (Prov. 14:34), then it is incumbent upon us to strive for the public acknowledgment of God.

LOOKING AHEAD

In these last few chapters, we've concentrated on *what* to say when engaging in expository apologetics. We've examined both the theology and the practice of apologetics, both classical/doctrinal apologetics issues and cultural/practical concerns. In the next chapter, we'll focus on *how* to say it. What are the mechanics of an expository apologetic encounter? And, having understood that, how do I then incorporate those principles into other encounters like preaching or teaching? These questions form the basis for the next two chapters, and for the application of the overall theory of expository apologetics to real life.

Basic Objections

While some objections to the faith focus on broader aspects of Christian belief, others go beyond the basics and home in on moral application. In other words, people usually get beyond questioning what Christianity *is* and start questioning what it *does*. In fact, conversations often start with the moral implications of Christian belief. This is partly because pragmatism is so prevalent in our culture. Most people don't care to know the *why*; they just want to get straight to the *what*.

In fact, I cannot remember the last time I had a conversation with a skeptic that fell exclusively into the classical apologetics category. Even at the highest level, atheists like Richard Dawkins, Sam Harris, and Christopher Hitchens argue more against the morality of Christianity than against its theology. The "New Atheism" is as much an attack on Christians and Christian ethics as it is an attack on Christian theology.

Today's atheists are greeted with rock-star status. Their books are far from being obscure titles assigned to graduate students in philosophy and apologetics, or relegated to the dustiest shelves of academic libraries; they have instead dominated best-sellers' lists.

As a result, we must be prepared to go beyond the questions that classical apologists faced in the past and to go where the rubber meets the road. Of course, classical questions are not somehow inferior or irrelevant. Most of us, however, will not be dealing with high-level philosophical thinkers and scholars. We will more likely find ourselves face-to-face with the person who wants to know why Christians have a problem with abortion or same-sex "marriage." And this will require us to be familiar with the moral law.

"WHY DO YOU KEEP SOME LAWS BUT NOT OTHERS?"

The best-known verse in the Bible used to be John 3:16. Rollen Stewart, the ubiquitous, "Rainbow Man" who wore John 3:16 signs at sporting events across the country "says he drove about 60,000 miles a year to attend events, and he got more TV face time than the network announcers who sometimes left him tickets."[1] More recently, University of Florida quarterback Tim Tebow championed the verse. In the same year that Tebow won the Heisman Trophy and led the Gators to a National Championship, he also revitalized the relationship between John 3:16 and the sports world.

However, as popular as John 3:16 was in the 1970s and '80s with the Rainbow Man, or the 2000s with Tim Tebow, it is still not the best-known verse in the conscience of the American culture. That distinction belongs to Matthew 7:1. Any Christian who has been in a discussion with an unbeliever about a controversial moral issue has more than likely been hit with the ever-so-popular "judge not lest ye be judged" line. Never mind that Jesus goes on to teach believers *how* to judge in verse 5, then again in verses 15–20. That is absolutely lost on those who rely on this "clobber verse."[2]

The good thing about Matthew 7:1 is that most Christians know how to deal with it. Or at least they catch on if you just walk them through the rest of the passage. There is, however, another verse that has grown in popularity in the world of cultural apologetics. Like Matthew 7:1, people use this verse in spite of the fact that they don't know where it is in the Bible. But unlike Matthew 7:1, people use this only as a passing reference to what "the Bible says somewhere." Moreover, this verse is not even a single verse; there are two of them! I know it sounds confusing, so allow me to explain.

When "don't judge me" is not enough, and it's time to pull out the big guns, opponents of biblical morality will often point to what they have been told is the hermeneutical inconsistency of adhering to part of the Old Testament law and leaving the rest. The "verse" that has come to represent this idea is not a verse at all; it is a sort of paraphrase that goes something like "shellfish is an abomination." Of course, this phrase does not occur in the Bible, but it is a reference to Leviticus 11:9–12 (cf. Deut. 14:10). And since it is difficult to deal with a verse that is not a verse, I'll handle this idea by using another verse that *is* an actual verse (and it's used almost as frequently): "You shall not round off the hair on your temples or mar the edges of your beard" (Lev. 19:27).

Again, people who refer to this verse rarely know where it is or what it actually says. However, our desire to be gracious with people requires us to go beyond nitpicking their inability to quote texts that we, quite frankly, couldn't quote ourselves. We know what they're talking about, and we should be prepared to respond. This is especially true when their argument has traction in the broader culture.

THE ARGUMENT GOES MAINSTREAM

In the second season of the TV show *The West Wing*, President Bartlet, played by Martin Sheen, obliterates a famous radio talk show host who insists on calling homosexuality an abomination. The woman (based on radio's Dr. Laura) stands there speechless while the president exposes her hypocrisy in what many on the left view as a classic example of prohomosexual "clobber passages" at work:

> "I'm interested in selling my youngest daughter into slavery as sanctioned in Exodus 21:7. She's a Georgetown sophomore, speaks fluent Italian, always cleaned the table when it was her turn. What would a good price for her be?
>
> "My chief of staff, Leo McGarry, insists on working on the Sabbath. Exodus 35:2 clearly says he should be put to death. Am I morally obligated to kill him myself or is it okay to call the police?
>
> "Here's one that's really important cause we've got a lot of sports fans in this town: touching the skin of a dead pig makes one unclean (Lev. 11:7). If they promise to wear gloves can the Washington Redskins still play football? Can Notre Dame? Can West Point?
>
> "Does the whole town really have to be together to stone my brother, John, for planting different crops side by side? Can I burn my mother in a small family gathering for wearing garments made from two different threads?
>
> "Think about those questions, would you?"[3]

The episode was a hit. Homosexual groups lauded its brilliance. Reliance on the "why do you pick and choose" attack gained traction.

Later, in 2008, California was considering controversial Proposition 8, which eventually passed, banning same-sex unions. Among the many efforts to rally people in favor of homosexual unions, several Hollywood stars, led by Jack Black, performed *Prop 8: The Musical*. In this short satirical piece, Black played the part of Jesus, and, once again, the "hypocritical use of the Levitical law" was the primary target:

JESUS, *spoken*. Well the Bible says a lot of things, y'know.

EVERYONE, *shouts*. Jesus Christ!

JESUS, *spoken*. Hey, how's it goin?

LEAD PROP 8 PROPONENT, *spoken*. Jesus, doesn't the Bible say these people are an abomination?

BLACK PROP 8 PROPONENT, *spoken*. Obamanation?

JESUS, *spoken*. Yeah but you know it says the exact same thing about this shrimp cocktail . . .

PROP 8 PROPONENTS, *spoken*. Mmm! Shrimp cocktail!

JESUS, *spoken*. Leviticus says shellfish is an abomination.

BLACK PROP 8 PROPONENT, *spoken*. Obamanation!

WOMAN WEARING PEACE SIGN, *spoken*. What else does the Bible say, Jesus?

JESUS, *spoken*. The Bible says a lot of interesting things.

JESUS, *sung*. Like you can stone your wife or sell your daughter into slavery.

LEAD PROP 8 PROPONENT, *spoken*. Well, we ignore those verses.

JESUS, *sung*. Well then friend it seems to me you pick and choose.

PROP 8 PROPONENTS, *sung*. We pick and choose!

JESUS, *sung*. Well, please choose love instead of hate, besides your nation was built on separation of church and state!

JESUS, *spoken*. See you later sinners!

Examples like this are myriad. I could list dozens. However, I share these two because of how strategic they are. The first was an episode in a long-running hit television series (the show ran for seven seasons). The second was an ad campaign in what was arguably the most strategic legal battle in the history of the fight for marriage. These are far from obscure cultural references. Nor were they debates in academic or political arenas. This is ground zero—the front lines in the battle in the marketplace of ideas. This is the perceived seat of power in the battle for hearts and minds. As such, there are at least three advantages to addressing these objections.

First, the fact that these arguments against biblical truth were so public demonstrates the amount of credence people gave them. Television shows are fiercely competitive and woefully unoriginal. Before something makes it to the air, it has usually been tested, studied, polled, evaluated, and reevaluated in an effort to score points with the target audience. The goal is not to alienate but to captivate the audience. Hence, we know that these are arguments in which people believe.

Second, the public and consistent nature of these attacks means that they work. The fact that Jack Black's character uses some of the exact same arguments that scored points on *The West Wing* eight years earlier indicates that these arguments are considered effective. Moreover, the latter was used in an effort to influence a public vote. And if the arguments work, they will show up in other arenas, and eventually they will become common fare among those striving to score points in this and other debates.

Third, if we can answer these objections, we will be prepared to deal with one of the most common obstacles facing modern apologists. Like a challenger who takes the champ's best shot early in a heavyweight fight and keeps coming forward, those who are able to withstand what the culture sees as a knockout blow to Bible-thumping Christians, and do so with poise and relative ease, will cause their assailants to pause and think twice before they throw another punch.

However, many Christians are stumped by this approach. The fact of the matter is that most Christians think the same thing when *they* read the Old Testament! We usually don't stress about it because we know we "are not under law but under grace" (Rom. 6:14). However, when we are dealing with issues like incest or bestiality, we find ourselves at a loss when people use these verses against us. On the one hand, we *know* such things are wrong and that the Bible makes that clear. On the other hand, we feel trapped because we also know (1) we are not under law, and (2) that's the only defense we have concerning the wrongness or sinfulness of these actions. It appears we're missing a step . . . or two.

But before we look at those missing steps, let's examine just why understanding the nature of the biblical law is so important to expository apologetics. Most obviously, this is important because expository apologetics is based on using Scripture as our primary and authoritative source for answering objections. And today that most certainly means responding to moral and ethical issues. Hence, it is inevitable that we will find ourselves referencing some of the verses in question.

Additionally, we must be aware that many people will view the mere fact that we are using the Bible at all as questionable. In other words, we are assuming that the Bible is the authority in a debate about whether such an authority exists. Some suggest that the best course of action is to abandon the Bible, at least for a time, until we can establish common ground. I say this is disastrous. Doing so would be an admission of defeat. Our interlocutors are allowed to keep their presuppositions regardless of where the conversation goes. If we abandon ours, we have conceded the most crucial point. We must do no such thing!

Instead of laying down our arms, we must show others that we are as armed as they are. Moreover, we must show them that their weapons look like ours in some very striking ways. We must show them that they, in fact, are using the very Bible they demand we lay down. And one way we can do this is by educating them in the law of God. Now back to those missing steps.

THREE TYPES OF LAW

We are indeed missing a few steps in the "you're picking and choosing" debate. First, we are missing a clear understanding of what is referred to commonly as the *threefold division of the law*. This is the idea that there is not just one type of law in the Old Testament; there are three. Nor is this something forced on the text. As you will see, these three types of law are obvious to anyone who will look at the Bible honestly and carefully.

Second, we are missing a basic grasp of God's law; we simply don't know it. Because we have been so steeped in ideas that undermine the concept of the perpetuity of the moral law, we have neglected to treat those laws as matters of first importance. Instead, we have opted for pragmatism and emotionalism. We soak in sermons that give us "Five

Ways to Avoid Temptation," but haven't a clue as to what constitutes sin. Moreover, we shun such doctrinal/theological subjects and consider them impractical and downright boring. The result is a brand of Christianity that looks almost nothing like that practiced by our forefathers.

For instance, the earliest Christian confessions and catechisms emphasized at least three things: (1) the basic metanarrative of creation-fall-redemption-consummation; (2) the Ten Commandments; and (3) the Lord's Prayer. In fact, two hundred years ago, one would have been hard-pressed to find someone running the streets of Europe or America who was unaware of these basic ideas. Today it's a different story.

Third, we are missing the hermeneutic that teaches that, as believers who are *not* under the law, we are to use the law in a lawful way, since "we know that the law is good, if one uses it lawfully" (1 Tim. 1:8). Again, this is of utmost importance if we believe, as I have argued, that the law is a useful and necessary tool in cultural apologetics. How shall we engage a culture that rejects the law of God if we don't believe in it ourselves, or know how to use it?

The Moral Law

The first and most significant kind of law is the transcendent, unchanging, ever-binding moral law. The moral law encompasses laws that have been and always will be the same for all people in all places and for all times. These laws reflect the very character of God. The Second London Confession states:

> The moral Law doth for ever bind all, as well justified persons as others, to the obedience thereof, and that not only in regard of the matter contained in it, but also in respect of the authority of God the Creator; who gave it: Neither doth Christ in the Gospel any way dissolve, but much strengthen this obligation.

These statements are worth examining closely.

First, "the moral law doth for ever bind all, as well justified persons as others, to the obedience thereof." As Philip Ross states, the moral law reveals "the demands of God upon all people, not just those in ancient Israel."[4] This, according to Ross, is due to the fact that "from the beginning they were the basis upon which God judged mankind. The coming of Christ and the incorporation of the Gentiles into the church did not nullify the [moral law]; it remains binding upon Christians and non-Christians alike."[5] Thus, Christian, non-Christian . . . it does not matter. The moral law is binding; it always has been, and it always will be. We will all stand before God and be judged for our deeds.

This is why God judges even pagan nations for violating his law:

> Do not make yourselves unclean by any of these things, for by all these the nations I am driving out before you have become unclean, and the land became unclean, so that I punished its iniquity, and the land vomited out its inhabitants. (Lev. 18:24–25)

Unfortunately, I have had to explain and defend the fact that the moral law applies to everyone to Christians more than unbelievers. It's as if someone has poisoned the well and started an epidemic that has Christians believing that God requires righteousness *only* of believers. I get questions such as, "Why are we surprised at the sinfulness of sinners?" and, "Why do we judge the behavior of those outside the church?" The idea behind these statements is that God has one standard of righteousness for Christians but another for the heathen. Leviticus 18 makes it clear that this is *not* the case! There is but one standard of righteousness, and all people and nations will be judged by that standard. This is also the message of Revelation 20:12–13:

> And I saw the dead, great and small, standing before the throne, and books were opened. Then another book was opened, which is the book of life. And the dead were judged by what was written in the books, according to what they had done. And the sea gave up the dead who were in it, Death and Hades gave up the dead who were in them, and they were judged, each one of them, according to what they had done.

Notice that it does not say that they are judged merely for rejecting Christ. They are judged for their deeds, and whether those deeds were righteous. Of course, there are no righteous deeds apart from Christ, thus everyone will miss the mark apart from him (Rom. 3:23). Nevertheless, we have a duty to call sinners to repent of their sin. As the prophet writes, "If I say to the wicked, 'You shall surely die,' and you give him no warning, nor speak to warn the wicked from his wicked way, in order to save his life, that wicked person shall die for his iniquity, but his blood I will require at your hand" (Ezek. 3:18; cf. 33:8, 14).

Let's take a closer look at another part of the statement from the Second London Confession: "and that not only in regard of the matter contained in it, but also in respect of the authority of God the Creator." In other words, God's moral law is not obeyed by accident. In order for an action to be righteous, it must be a right action, done the right way, for the right reason (the glory of God). Men owe God their obedience *and* their worship. A man who doesn't commit adultery simply because he fears the consequences or the social taboo has not obeyed God; he is not righteous. Righteousness is God's goodness.

Third, "neither doth Christ in the Gospel any way dissolve, but much strengthen this obligation." This is exactly what Jesus does in the Sermon on the Mount when he repeats the statement, "You have heard it said, but I say . . ." (Matt 5:21, 27, 33, 38, 43). He went beyond mere adherence to the letter of the law to the heart of the matter. He raised the stakes, so-to-speak, on the law of Moses. Hence, Christians "strive for peace with everyone, and for the holiness without which no one will see the Lord" (Heb. 12:14).

Christians often disagree about the perpetuity of the moral law. It is not my intention to solve that disagreement here; I merely want to acknowledge it. I stand in the Reformed, confessional tradition and hold to the perpetuity of the moral law. However, one need not agree with me in order to see the benefit of the moral law in expository apologetics. One need only recognize the current cultural climate and the need for clarity on issues that are condemned in the Bible, and often only in the Old Testament.

For example, Leviticus 18:6–18 defines and condemns incest. Thus, if one wishes to make a biblical argument against the practice, it is important to refer to this passage. However, doing so without distinguishing between moral and civil laws (which we will examine shortly) is exactly what leads to the "why do you condemn *this* and not *that*" charge leveled so frequently against those of us who believe in the authority of God's Word. And, lest you think this example of incest is a stretch, here are two headlines from recent stories out of the United Kingdom and Australia. The first headline reads: "Grandmother and Grandson to Have Child Together: A 72-Year-Old Grandmother Is to Have a Child with Her Grandson."[6] This story from the *Telegraph* continues:

> Pearl Carter and Phil Bailey, 26, have paid a surrogate mother £20,000 to have Mr Bailey's child, which the couple plan to bring up together.
>
> Mrs Carter, from Indiana, met Mr Bailey four years ago after he tracked her down following the death of his mother, Lynette.
>
> Mrs Carter fell pregnant with Lynette at 18, out of wedlock, and claims that she was forced to give her child up for adoption by her strict Catholic parents.
>
> She went on to marry, but never had any more children.
>
> The couple, who claim to be abused in public and could face prison for incest, say that they fell in love and became lovers soon after meeting.

Before you say, "That is just one sick, isolated incident," ask yourself a question: on what basis do you consider it sick? On what basis would the culture at large be able to call it sick? To what moral standard would they appeal?

While this story is bizarre and disturbing, the story out of Australia is more concerning since it lays the groundwork for a sea change in the legal/moral landscape: "Australian Judge Says Incest May No Longer Be a Taboo."[7] The story continues:

> Judge Garry Neilson, from the district court in the state of New South Wales, likened incest to homosexuality, which was once regarded as criminal and "unnatural" but is now widely accepted. . . . He said incest was now only a crime because it may lead to abnormalities in offspring but this rationale was increasingly irrelevant because of the availability of contraception and abortion.

There it is in black and white: a judge taking the argument for same-sex "marriage" to its logical and philosophical conclusion. If our standard of morality is based solely on negative consequences, and we can eliminate those consequences, then incest is no longer immoral. However, note that the judge begs a question. His assertion is based on the assumption that abortion is also no longer immoral! This is a real-life example of what happens when we assume the irrelevance of the moral law.

The Moral Law and the Decalogue

Where, then, do we find the moral law? The idea that the moral law is summed up in the Ten Commandments is as old as the Bible, itself.[8] Since the Reformation, this idea has been reiterated in virtually every Reformed confession and catechism. For example:

Westminster Shorter Catechism (1647):

> Q. 40. What did God at first reveal to man for the rule of his obedience?
> A. The rule which God at first revealed to man for his obedience was the moral law (Rom. 2:14–15; 5:13–14).

> Q. 41. Where is the moral law summarily comprehended?
> A. The moral law is summarily comprehended in the Ten Commandments (Deut. 10:4; Matt. 19:17).

The Catechism for Babes, or Little Ones (1652) summarized the idea this way:

> Q. What is sin?
> A. Sin is any naughtiness against any of Gods ten commands.

Heidelberg Catechism (1563):

> Q. 92. What is the law of God?
> A. God spake all these words [Exodus 20:1–17 and Deuteronomy 5:6–21] . . .

Instructions for the Ignorant (Bunyan's Catechism, 1675):

> Q. 36. What is sin?
> A. It is a transgression of the law (1 John 3:4).

Q. 37. A transgression of what law?
A. Of the law of our nature, and of the law of the Ten Commandments as written in the holy Scriptures (Rom. 2:12–15; Exodus 20).

Benjamin Keach's Catechism (1693):

Q. 46. What did God at first reveal to man for the rule of his
obedience?
A. The rule which God at first revealed to man for his obedience was
the moral law (Rom. 2:14–15; 5:13–14).

Q. 47. Where is the moral law summarily comprehended?
A. The moral law is summarily comprehended in the Ten Commandments (Deut. 10:4; Matt. 19:17).

A Catechism for Girls and Boys (1789)

Q. 34. How many commandments did God give on Mt. Sinai?
A. Ten commandments (Ex. 20:1–17; Deut. 5:1–22).

Q. 35. What are the ten commandments sometimes called?
A. God's moral law (Luke 20:25–28; Rom. 2:14–15; 10:5).

The Baptist Catechism (1813)

Q. 40. What did God at first reveal to man for the rule of his
obedience?
A. The rule which God at first revealed to man for his obedience,
was the moral law (Rom. 2:14–15, and 10:5).

Q. 41. Where is the moral law summarily comprehended?
A. The moral law is summarily comprehended in the ten commandments (Deut. 10:4; Matt. 19:17).

Time and space do not permit me to list every example of Reformed
catechesis cementing this idea in the minds of believers throughout
the centuries. However, this selected list serves two purposes. First,
I want the reader to know that the distinction between moral, civil,
and ceremonial law is far from a novel idea. Second, as I argued in
the previous chapter, catechism is one of the chief tools of expository
apologetics.

The Ceremonial Law

Leviticus 19:27 falls under the category of law frequently referred to as "ceremonial law." In fact, this is true of many of the laws referenced by our detractors. Whether it is the law of not eating shellfish, not sowing two types of seed in a field, or not using two types of thread in a garment, they all fall in the category of ceremonial law. These are the laws given to Israel for the express purpose of showing them what was holy in terms of worship. According to the Second London Baptist Confession:

> God was pleased to give to the people of Israel Ceremonial Laws, containing several typical ordinances, partly of worship, prefiguring Christ, his graces, actions, sufferings, and benefits; and partly holding forth divers instructions of moral duties, all which Ceremonial Laws being appointed only to the time of reformation, are by Jesus Christ the true Messiah and only Law-giver who was furnished with power from the Father, for that end, abrogated and taken away.[9]

These laws worked two ways. First, they told Israel what they must do to worship God and how to do it. Second, it told them what they were not to do in regard to worship. The law concerning the cutting of the beard in Leviticus 19:27 falls under the second category. As Jamieson, Fausset, and Brown observe:

> It seems probable that this fashion had been learned by the Israelites in Egypt, for the ancient Egyptians had their dark locks cropped short or shaved with great nicety, so that what remained on the crown appeared in the form of a circle surrounding the head, while the beard was dressed into a square form. This kind of coiffure had a highly idolatrous meaning; and it was adopted, with some slight variations, by almost all idolaters in ancient times. (Jeremiah 9:25, 26; 25:23, where "in the utmost corners" means having the corners of their hair cut.) Frequently a lock or tuft of hair was left on the hinder part of the head, the rest being cut round in the form of a ring, as the Turks, Chinese, and Hindus do at the present day.[10]

Hence, this law was designed to teach Israel not to worship Yahweh in ways similar to the worship practices of those who surrounded them.

The connection to idolatry becomes increasingly clear in light of the next verse: "You shall not make any cuts on your body for the dead or tattoo yourselves: I am the LORD" (Lev. 19:28). Clearly this is a reference to pagan worship practices from which Israel was required to flee. Hence, these laws, and others like them, were not universal in their implementation. They are, however, based on the application of the moral law, which helps us interpret them. As a result, they are not completely useless to us as they do teach us about holiness and acceptable worship. And *that* is an idea that is not limited to the Old Covenant (see Rom. 12:1; Phil. 4:18; Heb. 12:28; 1 Pet. 2:5).

The Civil/Judicial Law

The third type of law God gave Israel was civil, or judicial, law. These are the laws that governed everyday life in the nation of Israel. Second London says of the civil law:

> To them also he gave sundry judicial Laws, which expired together with the state of that people, not obliging any now by virtue of that institution; their general equity only, being of moral use.

Hence it would be wrong to attempt to apply the civil law universally. Doing so would be like taking the laws that govern driving in England (where they drive on the left side of the road) and importing them directly to the United States. Certainly there are similarities and common underlying principles that govern driving in both places. However, there are significant differences that would make such an adaptation impossible.

The same is true of Israel's civil laws. One cannot simply take the laws of a theocratic nation in the ancient Near East and apply them to modern societies without some significant caveats. For example:

> When you reap the harvest of your land, you shall not reap your field right up to its edge, neither shall you gather the gleanings after your harvest. And you shall not strip your vineyard bare, neither shall you gather the fallen grapes of your vineyard. You shall leave them for the poor and for the sojourner: I am the LORD your God. (Lev. 19:9–10)

The gleaning laws of ancient Israel were designed to care for the poor. These laws were designed with a culture in mind that was almost exclusively agrarian. It is obvious that applying such a law today would (1) fail to meet the needs of the poor and (2) put an undue burden on those whose livelihood consisted of farming. However, a number of principles in these laws can be applied

It would be wrong to merely throw out laws like the one above simply because they cannot be applied directly. God has not stopped caring for the poor. Nor should his people. Thus, it would be appropriate to refer to this law in an effort to determine how we should minister to the poor if we first examined the way it is used in the New Covenant (see 1 Timothy 5, for example). This is what the confession means by "their general equity only, being of moral use."

THE DISTINCTION BETWEEN THESE
LAWS IS UNCLEAR AT TIMES

> While "division" generally describes this framework for interpretation of the law, it need not be interpreted in the strongest terms. Whether the reference is to the law or to an army, "division" does not necessarily imply disunity. In some contexts, it merely highlights different categories and functions of the one thing.[11]

Knowing the difference between laws that are civil, ceremonial, or moral is the key to handling the "you pick and choose" argument. That is not to say that people will lay down their arms and acknowledge defeat when you show them that picking and choosing is wise, necessary, consistent, and logical. On the contrary, only the gospel changes hearts, and that is not the gospel. However, it will go a long way toward forcing them to acknowledge their own picking and choosing, and cause them to come up with an explanation as to why it's ok for them to do it and not us (more on this below). Two things will be helpful in moving such a conversation forward. First, it will be helpful to look at the preface to the codes of Leviticus 18:

> And the LORD spoke to Moses, saying, "Speak to the people of Israel and say to them, I am the LORD your God. You shall not do as they do in the land of Egypt, where you lived, and you shall not do as they do in the land of Canaan, to which I am bringing you. You shall not walk in their statutes. You shall follow my rules and keep

my statutes and walk in them. I am the LORD your God. You shall therefore keep my statutes and my rules; if a person does them, he shall live by them: I am the LORD." (vv. 1–5)

Notice the emphasis on Israel's separation from the pagans around them. The goal was that the Israelites would "not do as they do in the land of Egypt." Nor were they to "do as they do in the land of Canaan." In short, Israel was to be distinct—set apart in their worship of Yahweh. He ends the preface with the familiar refrain: "I am the LORD." This is the foundation of Israel's righteousness, and ours. It also goes a long way in explaining why certain laws in the Levitical Code make no sense outside the context of the ancient Near East. That is, unless they are interpreted in light of their intended purpose.

Second, it will be helpful to look at a section of the codes that contain elements with which our interlocutors will agree and disagree. This will create a situation where your challenger will be forced to relinquish his presumption of superiority. For example, let's look at Leviticus 18:19–23:

You shall not approach a woman to uncover her nakedness while she is in her menstrual uncleanness. And you shall not lie sexually with your neighbor's wife and so make yourself unclean with her. You shall not give any of your children to offer them to Molech, and so profane the name of your God: I am the LORD. You shall not lie with a male as with a woman; it is an abomination. And you shall not lie with any animal and so make yourself unclean with it, neither shall any woman give herself to an animal to lie with it: it is perversion.

This passage contains five prohibitions. Placing these prohibitions in order will help make the point:

1. No sex during menstruation (v. 19)
2. No adultery (v. 20)
3. No child sacrifice (v. 21)
4. No sodomy (v. 22)
5. No zooerasty/beastiality (v. 23)

When I ask people whether they would rather "pick and choose" from this list or live in a society where anything on it was fair game, they inevitably opt for the former as opposed to the latter. This, in turn, opens the discussion in fascinating and rewarding ways. No longer can our interlocutor view the discussion from the perspective of moral superiority due to what he perceives as our inconsistency and "picking and choosing." Now the ground is level. Or, at least they think it is, until they realize that while you were making a conscientious choice based on a cogent hermeneutic, *they* were the ones making arbitrary choices based on cultural whims and personal preferences.

As noted before, this is not enough to close the deal. This is merely another opening for the gospel, a chance to sprint to the cross. This is a moment where we can point to the fact that we do not trust ourselves to be the arbiter of truth. This is when we can point to our own sin and how it drove us to the Savior. Here is where we trust the Holy Spirit to reach into their chest and squeeze until they realize that they are arrogant, prideful, and idolatrous, and that they stand condemned before a holy and righteous God. Yes, this is the goal of the expository apologist! It is not enough to turn the tables and gloat over a "gotcha" moment. Our goal is the gospel. Our great joy is not in showing people their error, but in God showing them his mercy as they flee to Christ.

In this chapter we have explored the importance of having an answer to the "Why do you pick and choose?" argument. In the next chapter, we will examine specific ways we employ the law in expository apologetic encounters once we've established the appropriateness of viewing the law through the lens of the threefold division.

The Expository
Apologetic Waltz

Imagine that you're in the midst of a heated conversation with someone who is advocating for a theological, political, or philosophical idea that is at odds with biblical Christianity. For now it doesn't matter what the idea happens to be. What does matter is this: are you ready to respond? Failure to do so will imply tacit agreement with, or surrender to, an idea that opposes the gospel. Unfortunately, that's our normal response. We sit there, hat in hand, running through scenarios and doubts.

"That's not right! I should say something," we think. Of course, unless you are one of those brash and brazen apologetic ninjas, this thought is usually followed by, "But I don't want to be a jerk." Or, perhaps, "I want to be relational, not combative." Sometimes, our response is a little more honest. "I know I should say something, but I'm not sure what to say, and he sounds really confident . . . he'll eat me alive!" By now, the conversation has moved on to another topic and going back to engage would be awkward.

Don't feel alone. We've all been there. I have conversations like that from time to time. No one wants to be "at war" all the time. We all want peaceful interactions. Nor does every idea need to be confronted. Often we have to "pick our battles." Otherwise, we will come across as crass, insensitive, arrogant jerks. No one wants to engage jerks in meaningful conversation. I would say, "You know who you are." But unfortunately, most people like that have no idea! They pride themselves on shutting others down. Trust me; I know all too well. I used to be exactly like that.

I had a sharp mind and a sharper tongue. I could tie people up in knots during a verbal dispute . . . and I loved it! However, other people did not. They would avoid meaningful discussion for fear that they would be shut down if they said something I didn't agree with, or if they said something that wasn't completely accurate or perfectly logical. The result was fewer and fewer encounters. I had to come to see that my approach was both sinful and counterproductive. So what is the alternative?

THE WALTZ

In many ways a conversation is like a dance. Two people find a common space, a common theme, and begin to move cooperatively (or not so cooperatively) toward mutual understanding. Of course, not all dances are created equal. In fact, some dances consist of two people walking onto the floor together only to take off doing their own thing, almost as if their "partner" is not even there. That is definitely not the kind of dance to which I am referring. I'm talking about more of a waltz.

For my money, the waltz is the quintessential dance. There is nothing more gracious, elegant, or stylish. The music starts: da-da-da-da dum . . . and couples glide across the floor in smooth, effortless, majestic rhythm. Every time I hear music with a 3/4 time signature, I think about a waltz. One-two-three, one-two-three, one-two-three. The man approaches the woman. He requests her accompaniment. She agrees, and he leads her around the floor.

There is another waltz with which I am quite taken. This waltz does not involve music or dancing. But make no mistake—there is a definite rhythm, and there are definite rules. And if you will remember the rhythm of this waltz, it will serve you well as you contend for the biblical world- and lifeview over against all others. This waltz is a three-step process that will aid you in responding to objections to the Christian faith, even when they are less than overt in nature. As in a waltz, you will need to gain the trust and permission of your partner, and engage with them as you glide around the floor. Therefore, you must know where you are going.

First, let's look at the general approach, then we'll look at some specific examples.

Shall We Dance?

I fly a great deal. In fact, I cover between one hundred thousand and one hundred and fifty thousand miles a year in the air. I love to fly. I am fascinated by the aerodynamics. It never ceases to amaze me when a big wide-body jet uses the laws of aerodynamics to defy (though temporarily) the laws of gravity. However, there is another aspect of flying that intrigues me. Flying is one of the few places where people share the same space for significant amounts of time and, if they wish, can engage in fascinating conversations with people they otherwise would never have met, and with whom they often have little or nothing in common, beyond the fact that they are headed to the same destination.

An airplane is also a perfect setting to demonstrate my point. Just because you are sharing space with someone, that doesn't mean you have permission to engage them in meaningful conversation—just as standing next to someone on a crowded dance floor doesn't mean you've definitely found a partner. I have sat next to people for hours and barely been able to crack the "hello, how are you?" barrier. I have found, though, that when I show interest in engaging in conversation, most people will at least give it a whirl.

One of the first things we must learn to do is ask people to engage with us. There are no tricks here. We just have to learn to be cordial and friendly. Striking up a conversation is often a simple matter of putting yourself out there and smiling at someone. Ask about their day, their family, their work. I'm not talking about glad-handing, like a politician seeking votes. I'm talking about being neighborly. You'd be surprised how many people are willing to engage in conversation if someone would just take the time and show some interest. I've even done this on the subway in New York. And if you can make it there (i.e., striking up a conversation) . . . well, you know the rest.

Once we've found a dance partner, it's time to dance. Now, to continue the waltz metaphor, we must take the floor and lead. Here is where expository apologetics differs from evangelism. If we were talking about evangelism, this is the point where I'd write something about the need to turn the conversation toward spiritual things and make an opening for your presentation of the gospel. However, that is not what we do with expository apologetics.

Don't get me wrong. I am all for evangelism. There is no doubt that we must preach the gospel and make disciples (Matt. 28:18–20). I am not suggesting for a moment that evangelism is anything less than a priority in our conversations with people. However, I am suggesting a more subtle, and I believe, more productive and natural way to get to the gospel. And it all begins with a statement made by our partner in this waltz.

At some point in a meaningful conversation, the person to whom you are speaking will make a truth claim. This truth claim is actually the beginning of the expository apologetic waltz. For example, the person next to you on the plane (or bus, train, car, park bench) might be reading a newspaper. You strike up a conversation that eventually turns to the news of the day. Perhaps you say, "Boy, that Obamacare sure is a mess." Or, "The weather sure has been unseasonably cold." Whatever it is, you've opened the door for the other person to make a truth claim. Or perhaps to counter one of your truth claims. In any case, he makes a statement of fact. And not just any statement of fact; he makes a statement that reveals the presuppositions of a worldview that stand in stark opposition to biblical truth. Thus begins the waltz.

For our purposes, we will use what may be the most common issue of contention in our culture today: same-sex "marriage." As we progress, we will address objections that I have actually encountered.

STEP 1: SHOW THEM THEIR WORLDVIEW IS INCONSISTENT

The first step in the expository apologetic waltz is to help our interlocutor see that he is in error. Let me say at the outset that this is not a matter of pouncing on people. Although we have to talk about it in calculated terms in order to understand the process, this is far from an ambush. This is a way of thinking, a strategy of interaction. It should be marked by "gentleness and respect" (1 Pet. 3:15) and "complete patience and teaching" (2 Tim. 4:2). Nevertheless, we must take advantage of every opportunity to help people see the truth.

People usually don't make assertions unless they think they're right. And the more committed they are to those assertions, the less likely they are to see the error in it. That's where we come in. Our job is to find a way to expose the error. In order to do this, we must listen carefully in order to summarize their position, then demonstrate the inconsistency and/or fallacy therein.

There is an assumption here. We can assume that all people, unless they are arguing from a biblical worldview/perspective, will have holes in their logic. We assume this because "the fear of the LORD is the beginning of knowledge" (Prov. 1:7). Moreover, we know that in Christ "are hidden all the treasures of wisdom and knowledge" (Col. 2:3). Therefore, the fool who believes there is no God (Prov. 14:1; 53:1) or claims to be wise apart from God (Rom. 1:22), will always be amiss in his assessment of the way things are. And if we listen long enough, and carefully enough, we will hear it.

Listen Carefully

In my opinion, listening is the most important and least appreciated skill in apologetics. As noted earlier, most people interested in apologetics love to hear themselves talk. Moreover, they are also used to being the smartest people in the room (or at least they think they are). And we know that "when words are many, transgression is not lacking, but whoever restrains his lips is prudent" (Prov. 10:19). This can make the act of listening quite a challenge for those of us interested in contending for the faith.

James's words are informative here: "Know this, my beloved brothers: let every person be quick to hear, slow to speak, slow to anger; for the anger of man does not produce the righteousness of God" (James 1:19–20). And, although it is not Scripture, there is much wisdom in the age-old saying, "God gave us two ears and one mouth so we can do twice as much listening as speaking." Listening to people is a function of our respect for them. If we believe people have value, that their ideas matter, then we will listen to them. "Do nothing from selfish ambition or conceit, but in humility count others more significant than yourselves" (Phil. 2:3). When we are dismissive of people, or when we don't respect them, their words mean little to us.

Roger Nicole, in an article entitled, "How to Deal with Those Who Differ from Us," uses the example of Cornelius Van Til to emphasize this point:

> In this respect, I say that Dr. Cornelius Van Til has given us a splendid example. As you may know, he expressed very strong objections to the theology of Karl Barth. This was so strong that Barth claimed that Van Til simply did not understand him. It has been my privilege to be at Dr. Van Til's office and to see with my own eyes the bulky tomes of Barth's, *Kirchliche Dogmatik* (Incidentally, these volumes were the original German text, not an English translation). As I leafed through these, I bear witness that I did not see one page that was not constellated with underlining, double-underlining, marginal annotations, exclamation points, and question marks galore. So here is someone who certainly did not say, "I know Karl Barth well; I understand his stance; I don't need to read anymore of this; I can move on with what I have." Every one of the volumes, including the latest ones that were then in existence, gave evidence of very, very careful scrutiny. So when we intend to take issue with somebody, we need to do the job that is necessary to know that person so that we are not voicing our criticism in the absence of knowledge but that we are proceeding from the vantage point of real acquaintance.[1]

The goal in our listening is understanding. We don't just want to "catch" people; we want to hear them. There's a reason they believe what they believe, and we want to know what it is. Moreover, we want them to know that we value them. This will be abundantly clear when we show them that we've been paying attention to what they've been saying.

Summarize Generously

One of the best communication practices I've learned is active listening.[2] Mortimer J. Adler's book, *How to Speak, How to Listen,* has been a mainstay since its publication in 1983. I was shocked when someone first recommended it to me in seminary. However, it has since become a trusted resource. Concerning the matter of active listening, Adler writes, "The most prevalent mistake that people make about both listening and reading is to regard them as passively receiving rather than as actively participating."[3] This, of course, is due to the fact that:

> Listening, like reading, is primarily an activity of the mind, not of the ear or the eye. When the mind is not actively involved in the process, it should be called hearing, not listening; seeing, not reading.[4]

Interestingly, our lack of attention to this detail is unique in its application. Again, Adler notes:

> [People] do not make this mistake about writing and speaking. They recognize that writing and speaking are activities that involve expenditures of energy, unflagging attention, and the effort to reach out to the minds of others by written or oral communication. They also realize that some persons are more skilled in these activities than others and that increased skill in their performance can be acquired by attention to rules of art and by putting the rules into practice so that skilled performance becomes habitual.[5]

Hence, we would do well to pay more attention to how we listen. And one of the elements of active listening is feedback. Feedback is one way to let people know that you are listening. It is also a great way to enhance your listening. In this way it serves a dual purpose. First, in order to give feedback, you have to listen with a view toward summarizing what you're hearing. This, in turn, makes you listen more carefully. Second, when you do give feedback, the other person is assured that you really are listening to what he is saying.

There is also another benefit. When you summarize what you've heard, it gives the other person an opportunity to restate his position. Sometimes people aren't clear. Giving them a summary of what they've said will help them see that. At other times, the fault lies at our feet. Perhaps we assumed something or misheard it. In either case, we have an opportunity to achieve greater clarity. This is of critical importance when considering the next step in the process.

Oppose Them Gently

Once we are sure we have heard and understood, it is time to respond. Here is where we must be especially careful. As my brother-in-law would say, here's where we have to proceed "like a woodpecker with a headache." Or, as the apostle Peter said:

> But in your hearts honor Christ the Lord as holy, always being prepared to make a defense to anyone who asks you for a reason for the hope that is in you; yet do it with gentleness and respect, having a good conscience, so that, when you are slandered, those who revile your good behavior in Christ may be put to shame. For it is better to suffer for doing good, if that should be God's will, than for doing evil. (1 Pet. 3:15–17)

This is particularly difficult for at least three reasons.

First, people are defensive. No one likes to be corrected. Especially by strangers. Who wants someone they barely know pointing out inconsistencies in their worldview? We don't even like strangers to tell us our fly is open. And that's for our immediate benefit! So we sure don't want to hear that our worldview is in the weeds.

Second, there's the eleventh commandment. Perhaps you're unfamiliar with the eleventh commandment, "Thou Shalt Be Nice." Interestingly, this is the only commandment that receives universal acceptance in our culture. Moreover, it is the only commandment whose application most people are willing to insist upon. Press for the fifth commandment and you may hear from child protective services. Mention the third commandment, and you're a prude who needs to lighten up. Herald the tenth, and you lack drive and ambition. However, speak up on behalf of the eleventh, and you are a true paragon of virtue!

This, of course, is not to say that we should be mean to people. The Bible is clear about that:

> The Lord's servant must not be quarrelsome but kind to everyone, able to teach, patiently enduring evil, correcting his opponents with gentleness. God may perhaps grant them repentance leading to a knowledge of the truth, and they may come to their senses and escape from the snare of the devil, after being captured by him to do his will. (2 Tim. 2:24–26)

However, the specific application of the eleventh commandment tends to apply to religious debate. The idea is that we should not confront people about their religious beliefs . . . unless, of course, those beliefs are traditional, Protestant, biblical beliefs. Then they're fair game, since those beliefs are inherent violations of the eleventh commandment.

Third, we don't like to do it. Let's be honest. We simply do not like to confront people. In fact, some of us would rather be slapped in the face than have to tell people their worldview is wrong. Nor is this necessarily a sign of weakness on the part of the Christian. Even the apostle Paul, at the end of his discourse on spiritual warfare, asked his fellow believers to pray that God would grant him boldness:

> To that end keep alert with all perseverance, making supplication for all the saints, and also for me, that words may be given to me in opening my mouth boldly to proclaim the mystery of the gospel, for which I am an ambassador in chains, that I may declare it boldly, as I ought to speak. (Eph. 6:18–20)

If Paul needed prayer in this regard, then certainly the rest of us do. But we can also use some encouragement, and a few reminders as well. So here are a few things to remember.

(1) Remember that you are not claiming to be better than the people to whom you are speaking. This is about worldview, not value. They are making a truth claim, and you have noticed inconsistencies. You are not saying you are better; you're just working toward mutual understanding.

(2) Remember that you are engaged in a conversation and your ideas and opinions have as much standing as theirs. While it is important not to be arrogant, it is just as important not to be reticent. The current politically correct climate is enough to strike fear into the heart of the most confident Christian. We hear time and again how intolerant we are, and that takes a toll. As a result, we have to remind ourselves that the expression of our faith is not a crime. Nor is it inherently impolite.

(3) Remember that your assignment is to be faithful . . . that is all. One surefire way to thwart your progress in these types of engagements is to assume the mantle of success. If you believe every engagement has

to end in triumph, you will find yourself disappointed and defeated. This process is not a question of your ability to change or convert someone. It's not even about your ability to convince people. It is simply a matter of taking advantage of an opportunity to converse with other human beings and to share with them the most important thing in your world. God will take care of the rest.

(4) Remember that this is just the first step in the process. That means we have to be "wise as serpents and innocent as doves" (Matt. 10:16). We want the conversation to continue, but we also want to make our point. As a result, we must be equal parts confident and careful.

Our Example: Same-Sex "Marriage"

So, what does this look like in real life? In my conversations with numerous people on the topic of same-sex "marriage," I have encountered the same objections over and over again. However, for our purposes, we will address the objection at the heart of the debate. This is the idea that "when two people love each other, they should be allowed to marry." Or, stated differently, "We should not deny people their basic human rights based solely on their sexual identity."

First, we listen carefully. This is very important for all the reasons stated earlier. However, it is even more important when the issue is so volatile and opinions are held so strongly. We have to make sure we are not putting words in people's mouths, or misstating their positions or intentions.

Second, we summarize generously. That means we don't offer opinion in our summary. We don't jump straight to, "So you're saying that men should marry sheep?" We say something like, "Is it your contention that this issue comes down to the fact that when two people love each other, we should allow them to marry no matter who they are?" And we allow them to offer either affirmation or correction. You will be surprised just how effective this can be. At times, simply hearing their statements repeated back to them will cause people to rethink their assertions.

Finally, we oppose gently. I have offered a number of lines of reasoning based on a number of factors (i.e., am I speaking to someone who self-identifies as homosexual?). But my general response is always designed to show people that their assertion is inconsistent because: (1) It requires the legislation of emotion. What about people who don't love each other? Can they marry? (2) It is discriminatory. What about people who love more than one other person? Doesn't your position discriminate against them? (3) It assumes that marriage to any person under any circumstance is a human right without actually proving the assertion.

At this point, step 1 is complete. The goal here is merely to demonstrate holes in the assertion. We will go further in the next step.

STEP 2: SHOW THEM WHERE THEY'RE COUNTERFEITING

All truth is God's truth. We've all heard that saying before; most of us have probably used it. But have you ever pondered it? "Every good gift and every perfect gift is from above, coming down from the Father of lights with whom there is no variation or shadow due to change" (James 1:17). The psalmist adds, "The sum of your word is truth" (Ps. 119:160). And Jesus prayed that the Father would "sanctify them in the truth; your word is truth" (John 17:17). Essentially, because God is God, he determines what is true. Therefore, there can be no truth beyond, above, or outside of God. As a result, whatever truth our dance partners affirm is a truth they stole from God.

Showing our interlocutors where they are counterfeiting will require discovering the biblical/theological source of the ideal they are promoting, citing that source in a way that will help them see that they are, in fact, counterfeiting the ideas of another, and then summarizing for them why this is in fact counterfeiting.

Find the Source

Let me say right off that this is the most difficult of the three steps. In this step, we go from being active listeners to being expository apologists. Here is where we have to have a grasp on the biblical worldview, creeds, confessions, catechisms, the moral law, and the Ten Commandments, and be able to apply it on the spot. This is why I have argued up to this point that we must prepare for expository apologetics. Remember, we are giving an answer for what we believe; therefore, we have to believe something first. I realize you may not be there yet, and that's quite all right. This is a long journey. For now, just try to grasp the concept.

When I refer to the "source" here, I am not suggesting we find the source from which the person learned his truth claim. That would be truly prohibitive. In fact, that would be almost impossible for him! I am referring here to the biblical source for his claim. And before you think I've taken leave of my senses, let me explain.

People are made in the image of God (Gen. 1:12–28). They also have consciences. As such, there is a sense in which we are all aware of God's law. Paul alludes to this in Romans 2 when he writes of the Gentiles, "They show that the work of the law is written on their hearts, while their conscience also bears witness, and their conflicting thoughts accuse or even excuse them" (Rom. 2:15). This is not to say that men automatically know the Decalogue. However, everyone has a sense of right and wrong. And, to the degree that this lines up with God's Word, it is true.

> For the wrath of God is revealed from heaven against all ungodliness and unrighteousness of men, who by their unrighteousness suppress the truth. For what can be known about God is plain to them, because God has shown it to them. For his invisible attributes, namely, his eternal power and divine nature, have been clearly perceived, ever since the creation of the world, in the things that have been made. So they are without excuse. (Rom. 1:18–20)

Thus, when people make truth claims, we can usually find the biblical reality to which they are referring even if they are completely unaware of it. Our job is to find the source even if they can't. Are they seeking equality among people? This is sourced in our having been made in the image of God. Are they seeking relief of the poor? Care for the widow, orphan, or foreigner? These things are all found in the biblical worldview. How about better stewardship of the environment? Again, the Bible is the source of a proper understanding of that.

Some issues apply more directly to the biblical narrative. Sometimes the truth claims we are dealing with are truth claims about the nature of God, the person and work of Christ, the creation of the cosmos, or the problem of evil and suffering. In these cases, the connection is much easier to make. However, the goal at this point remains the same. We need to identify the biblical source for the truth they are attempting to argue.

Cite the Source

Once we have found the source of the truth claim, the next step is to cite it. In other words, we need to let people know where it comes from. We want to frame the conversation as their worldview versus the biblical worldview as opposed to their opinion versus our opinion. This is not a battle of wills. Nor can we simply "agree to disagree." This is a matter of God having spoken.

This does not mean that we have to cite book, chapter, and verse. However, it wouldn't hurt to do so. The point here is to let our inter- locutor know that we are appealing to a source outside ourselves. In fact, I believe it is important to make that very point. I like to tell people in no uncertain terms that I do not believe I am a sufficient source of truth anymore than I believe they are. I am just one beggar telling an- other beggar where I found bread. However, this goes back to the issue of presuppositions. Therefore, we must keep a couple of things in mind.

First, remember that everyone has presuppositions. In fact, this ver- bal waltz can be characterized as a dance of presuppositions. The main difference, however, is that those of us who take the time to examine our presuppositions will often find that having done so puts us in rare company. Rarely will you encounter people who know what their pre- suppositions are, let alone where they come from. That is why it is incumbent upon us to inform them.

Second, remember that people don't like having their presupposi- tions challenged. It can be a very uncomfortable process. Hence, we need to be very careful and go slow. Like a woodpecker with a headache.

Our Example: Same-Sex "Marriage"

We have established that the basic truth claim upon which the same- sex "marriage" advocate bases his claim is the idea that "when two people love each other, they should be allowed to marry." Or, stated another way, "We should not deny people basic human rights simply because they are homosexual." What, then, is the biblical truth at the core of this argument? What is the "good thing" that has been applied wrongly? Is it not the idea that there are certain rights that should not or cannot be denied? Now we've found the source.

This is most certainly a truth a Christian can embrace. It is a biblical truth. A brief survey of the second table of the law would confirm this. We could point, for example, to both the sixth and eighth commandments as examples that undergird this idea. Now we have cited the source.

A more careful look at the prohibitions against murder and theft shows that they support very clearly the idea that it is wrong to deny a person's basic right to life and private property. It is wrong to murder someone because of their basic right to life. And it is wrong to steal from another because of their basic right to private property. Now we have summarized the source.

However, there's another step. It is one thing to tell a person that the Bible supports their idea. It is quite another thing to tell them that their idea is an inferior knockoff. Remember, our goal here is to show our interlocutors that they are arguing for a good thing from a flawed worldview, and, as a result, they have turned a good thing into a wrong thing. In this case, we need to help them see that while the idea of not denying people basic rights is a good thing, the assumption that such rights include a man's right to marry another man, or a woman's right to marry another woman, is a horse of a different color.

Their version of rights has at least three major problems. First, they have no boundaries. Are we talking about any "two people"? If so, why? On what basis do we discriminate against three, four, or five people who want to enter into a consensual union? Doesn't the person with the bisexual "orientation" deserve the same rights as the same-sex couple seeking marriage? And if that right is based on no more than a person being able to marry based solely on their personal feelings and desires (i.e., their "orientation"), then failure to allow the bisexual to enter a polyamorous triad is clearly discriminatory.

The second problem with their version of rights is that it has its origin in man and not God. Even the term "human rights" has an air of hubris. Men do not make themselves. They can't even keep themselves alive. There is obviously a power greater than man, and we are all accountable to him.

Finally, their version of rights infringes on the rights of others (for example, people who want to marry more than one person, or a non-person) and, therefore, violates its own premise. What if one of them is already married? What if one of them is fifty and the other fifteen? Aren't we discriminating in these cases? And if we are, how, then, can we claim the moral high ground?

STEP 3: SHOW THEM WHAT THE REAL THING LOOKS LIKE

Up to this point, we have shown our interlocutors where their worldview is inconsistent. We have also shown them that the best and truest aspect of their truth claim is rooted in truth that is part of the biblical worldview. Now in the final step of this verbal waltz we demonstrate the consistency, superiority, and beauty of the Christian worldview.

We Must Explain Why the Christian Worldview Is True

We must explain why the truth is . . . well, true. In order to do this, we don't have to convince others. In fact, we cannot do that. That is the job of the Holy Spirit. Our job is simply to give a reason for the hope that is in us. We must explain why *we* have come to accept the truth, and why it is reasonable to do so.

This requires more than saying, "Well, God said it, I believe it, and that settles it." We need to explain our presuppositional claims. Let them know that we have presuppositions just like they do. And we need to show the consistency of those claims. For instance, the most popular sermon I've ever preached is titled, "Why I Choose to Believe the Bible." The short version is: "The Bible is a reliable collection of historical documents, written by eyewitnesses during the lifetime of other eyewitnesses; they report supernatural events that took place in fulfillment of specific prophesies, and claim that their writings are divine rather than human in origin." Of course, there is more to it than that (otherwise it would be a very short sermon). However, this portion gets to the heart of the matter.

We Must Explain Why the Christian Worldview Is Better

Our position is better because it is rooted in a timeless, perfect, external source. People are flawed. Every aspect of our person, our thinking, our reasoning, our desires, our motives is flawed. As a result, we cannot trust our own opinions when it comes to matters as important as worldview. Moreover, different people have different opinions, and without some timeless, perfect, external standard, we're reduced to engaging in some form of a duel to determine whose standard reigns supreme. In that case, the person who is smarter, more articulate, bigger, stronger, more intimidating, or simply connected to more political power becomes the one whose standard reigns supreme. This is an untenable position.

Our position is also better because it conforms to God's unchanging standard of righteousness. God is God. This may sound reductionistic. However, it is true. God is not running for God. And he has revealed himself to us. He has not left us wandering aimlessly through the world hoping we stumble upon the true, the good, and the beautiful. God has spoken, and we are obligated to listen. Thus, the position that is reached by virtue of such presuppositions is better than one that is not.

Our position is better because it is of greatest benefit to people made in the image of God. Humanity is not the product of random processes. We are made in the image of God. As such, it is of great benefit for us to order our lives in keeping with God's Word.

We Must Explain Why Worldview Matters

It is one thing for our position to be true and better. It is another thing to argue that it is of consequence, that in the end it actually matters. Here is where we "get to the gospel" in our expository apologetic. This is our opportunity to talk about the reason behind our reason, the truth behind our truth.

It matters because God is real.
It matters because God is righteous.
It matters because judgment is coming.

Our Example: Same-Sex "Marriage"

Returning to the same-sex "marriage" debate, we can now complete our case. We have established that (1) the idea that "people who love each other should be allowed to marry" is untenable since it relies on assumptions that cannot be sustained, and (2) the desire for people to be treated equally is an idea rooted in Scripture, but absent in the worldview behind same-sex "marriage." Now it's time to demonstrate that the biblical worldview is superior in its application of the truth in question.

One reason the biblical position is superior is its consistency. The biblical position offers the same rights to all people, whereas the alternative attempts to offer special rights to some people (homosexuals) while denying those rights to others (polygamists, polyamorists, pedophiles, etc.), all while claiming "equality" as its central goal. Today, homosexuals have the right to marry. There is no test for a couple applying for a marriage license to determine if one of them has same-sex attraction. In fact, no such test exists. There are homosexuals who are married. The news is filled with stories of people who "come out" to their spouse. Note that this does not end their marriage automatically. No one comes in and says, "You are homosexual; you cannot be married!" What homosexuals do not have is the right to redefine marriage to include people of the same sex. In other words, they can marry; they just cannot redefine marriage.

Another reason the biblical position is superior is its compatibility with history, science, and religion. Marriage was defined long ago. It is a union between the two halves of humanity. It is built on the idea of complementary parts coming together to form a family unit for the procreation, protection, and provision necessary for children to thrive. There is a reason that this idea has been around thousands of years. There is also a reason it is part of American law and culture. It is based on the biblical framework that gave us our laws—without which our laws make no sense.

A final reason the biblical position is superior is that it is . . . biblical! It is in keeping with what God has revealed. It is aligned with the picture Paul paints in Ephesians 5 of the relationship between man and wife as a metaphor for the relationship between Christ and his church.

There are other reasons that could be enumerated here. However,

I'm providing just one example of what expository apologetic encounters look like. And, as you can see here, they are not all that complicated. This is especially true when we remember the goals stated earlier. We are not out to paint people into intellectual corners or tie them in knots. Our goal is to expose their presuppositions and explain our own.

LOOKING AHEAD

While engaging in one-on-one conversations is the heart of expository apologetics, our efforts do not end there. The nature of the approach lends itself to teaching and preaching as well. In the next chapter, we will examine ways to turn any lesson or sermon into an opportunity for expository apologetics.

Preaching and Teaching Like an Expository Apologist

Expository apologetics is an incredible tool for personal encounters with skeptics. As we have seen, this method is designed for honest, meaningful interaction. It is based on the notion that all believers are apologists, whether they know it or not—and whether they want to be or not. It is also based on the idea that our entire Christian discipleship ought to be, in one sense, preparation for apologetics, which is about knowing what we believe and why we believe it, and being able to communicate that belief to a curious world in a winsome manner.

However, there is another aspect of expository apologetics that separates it from other approaches. A clue to this difference is contained in the adjective *expository*. This method is essentially a vehicle for exposition, for proclamation. As such, expository apologetics is built for preaching and teaching. In fact, for me, that's where the method was born! It wasn't until a friend mentioned the fact that I had a habit of "doing apologetics in my sermons" that I began to evaluate what I was doing.

Then a student of mine challenged me to codify and systematize my "method." He noticed that my sermons and lectures were filled with what he called "arguments" or "conversations" with doubters. As I pointed out in the introduction, I would make a point, then say something like, "I know what you're thinking . . ." Then I would express a common objection to the claim I was making and answer the objection.

It wasn't something I'd been taught. It was just the way I thought about the Bible. I was a skeptic. I remember what it was like to doubt, and I always assume that there are people like me in the audience.

Once I became aware of this practice, I began to analyze it. I also tried to be more purposeful about it. After that, I began to teach it to young preachers I mentored, until, finally, one of them challenged me to write this book. Thus, it is only fitting that we devote this last chapter to the application of this method to the act of proclamation.

But the goal here is to go beyond the pastor/teacher. This is also for the Sunday school teacher who prepares lessons week in and week out. This is also for the parent raising children in the discipline and instruction of the Lord (Eph. 6:4), or the older man or woman in the faith making disciples among their younger or less mature brothers and sisters (Titus 2). No matter the circumstance, anyone engaged in opening the Word of God and expounding on it needs to be adept at expository apologetics.

Nor is the goal here to give an instructional on preaching and teaching, per se. The nuts and bolts of expository apologetics are the same here as they are in the individual encounter to which we have given so much attention to this point. This chapter is not so much about how to preach and teach as it is about how to prepare our sermons and lessons with the expository apologetic angle in mind. In essence, this is about learning to see the expository apologetic opportunities inherent in every passage.

PREACHING AND EXPOSITORY APOLOGETICS

I hate movie preaching . . . I just hate it! More often than not, preachers in the movies are either mystics—milk-toast, self-help, pop-psychology-spouting sissies—or they are hyped-up motivational speakers calling their audience to "be all they can be." It is as though Hollywood knows nothing of biblical preaching. Either that, or they know it will offend the sensibilities of their audience. In either case, the preaching represented in the culture at large is woefully inadequate. Preaching is about more than helping people cope or motivating them to try harder. Preaching is an extraordinary act where a man stands suspended between two worlds holding forth truths that must be believed by an audience that, in and of themselves, cannot and will not believe unless the world they inhabit is invaded by the world that was and is and is to come.

For this reason, I believe every sermon ought, in part, to be an exercise in expository apologetics. This is true for at least three reasons. First, like expository apologetics, preaching is an act of persuasion. The preacher's goal is not merely to inform. Preaching is about calling for response. The preacher is called to "reprove, rebuke, and exhort, with complete patience and teaching" (2 Tim. 4:2). We are to be like Paul, who "tried to persuade Jews and Greeks" (Acts 18:4). This is the heart of preaching. "Therefore, knowing the fear of the Lord, we persuade others" (2 Cor. 5:11).

Second, expository apologetics is a vital part of preaching because "we preach Christ crucified, a stumbling block to Jews and folly to Gentiles" (1 Cor. 1:23). We must always remember that "the word of the cross is folly to those who are perishing" (1 Cor. 1:18). Hence, we cannot assume that those who hear us will believe. We must assume that our audience will have questions, and we must offer a reasoned response.

Third, even believers wrestle with unbelief. People must be persuaded because (1) they suppress the truth in unrighteousness, (2) they continue to battle sin even after being converted, and (3) they are engaged in a spiritual battle with the world, the flesh, and the Devil. As such, believers are tempted constantly to forsake the truth they know. Expository apologetics is a means by which we can aid them in this fight. By preaching to the doubt, disbelief, and confusion, we are constantly calling God's people back to him and his truth.

Read Your Text Like a Skeptic. Try to put yourself in the place of a person who does not assume the truth of what you are saying. How would they hear this text? What objections would they raise? What would they misunderstand? What would offend them? Confuse them? You will be surprised how helpful this simple practice can be in terms of changing your perspective on a text and how to teach it.

Argue with Yourself. One of the challenges I give myself as I am making proclamations in my sermons is, "Prove it!" It is easy to look at a text and see its meaning. However, communicating its meaning to a hostile audience is a different thing altogether. Arguing with yourself brings the hostile audience into your study, which is important since they will likely be present when you preach.

Preach to *People . . . Not at Them.* Young preachers often tend to preach as if their sermons were for their preaching professor as opposed to the Sunday morning audience. The result is heady, technically sound sermons that absolutely do not connect with people where they live. We must remember that preaching is supposed to be persuasive in nature. As the apostle Paul says, "Therefore, knowing the fear of the Lord, we persuade others" (2 Cor. 5:11). This means that we do not merely inform; we preach with a view toward changing minds and seeing God change hearts.

Expository apologetics is not about answering esoteric objections. This is real live, rubber-meets-the-road stuff. This is supposed to be a staple of our everyday preaching and teaching (Titus 1:9), and it ought to characterize our basic approach to presenting the gospel (1 Pet. 3:15; Jude 1–4). Hence, we must begin with basic, everyday objections. But where do we find those objections?

PERSONAL OBJECTIONS

The first step in discovering what kinds of objections to our message people might have is to not assume anything. That may sound simple enough, but when it comes to interpreting and teaching the Bible, it's more than a notion. We bring myriad presuppositions to the text and to the teaching/preaching encounter. These assumptions include what we know, what our listeners know, the clarity and effectiveness of our thinking and communication, and the receptivity of our audience, to name just a few. And while it is impossible to divorce ourselves completely from our assumptions, it is possible to confront them more effectively.

Allow me to recommend the following four steps as a starting place:

(1) We must not assume we know what the Bible says. How many times have you read a familiar passage only to find that you've either inserted or eliminated words or complete phrases? A classic example is Matthew 23:37 (cf. Luke 13:34), where Jesus says, "O Jerusalem, Jerusalem, the city that kills the prophets and stones those who are sent to it! How often would I have gathered your children together as

a hen gathers her brood under her wings, and you were not willing!" I've heard preachers read this text and still misquote it! They say, "How often would I have gathered *you* as a hen gathers her brood under her wings?" In fact, I've read this in a published book even after the author was challenged on it! The implication, of course, is that Jesus wanted to gather the people, but they were unwilling to be gathered. This, however, is not what the text says.

If you want to test yourself, try to look up biblical passages using an electronic source. I cannot tell you how many times I've put a phrase in a search column only to discover that it doesn't exist anywhere in the Bible! Of course, when I tweak my search, I usually find that I was off by a word or two. However, sometimes a word or two can be the difference between truth and heresy. We simply must read the Bible carefully and stop assuming that we know what it says.

(2) We must not assume we know what the Bible means. Closely related to our assumption about our accuracy concerning the Bible's content is our unwarranted confidence in our grasp of the Bible's meaning. I'm not talking about the perspicuity of Scripture or the Bible's ability to be understood. I'm referring to our arrogance in assuming that our understanding is not only correct but complete.

"Do your best to present yourself to God as one approved, a worker who has no need to be ashamed, rightly handling the word of truth" (2 Tim. 2:15). These words drive us onward in pursuit of our high calling. As Paul has explained elsewhere, "For we are not, like so many, peddlers of God's word, but as men of sincerity, as commissioned by God, in the sight of God we speak in Christ" (2 Cor. 2:17). Nor is this true only of those who hold office and teach others. This is the pursuit of every child of God who desires to be conformed to the image of our Savior: "Like newborn infants, long for the pure spiritual milk, that by it you may grow up into salvation—if indeed you have tasted that the Lord is good" (1 Pet. 2:2–3).

This kind of pursuit does not mark those who assume they know all there is to be known. This is the passionate pursuit of those who echo the sentiment of Job, who "would seek God, and to God would I commit my cause, who does great things and unsearchable, marvelous things without number" (Job 5:8–9). It is this kind of humble, passionate pursuit that is fitting for those who preach "the unsearchable riches of Christ, and to bring to light for everyone what is the plan of the mystery hidden for ages in God who created all things" (Eph. 3:8–9). Let us say with the psalmist, "I will meditate on your precepts and fix my eyes on your ways. I will delight in your statutes; I will not forget your word" (Ps. 119:15–16).

(3) We must not act as if we've never been lost. "But thanks be to God, that you who were once slaves of sin have become obedient from the heart to the standard of teaching to which you were committed, and, having been set free from sin, have become slaves of righteousness" (Rom. 6:17–18). Do you remember what it was like to be a slave to sin? Do you remember unrighteousness? Do you remember doubt? Sometimes we become so far removed from our past (which can be good) that we forget it (which can be bad). If we're not careful, this can make us jaded and calloused when relating to people struggling with real questions that require real answers.

Remember, friend, "we ourselves were once foolish, disobedient, led astray, slaves to various passions and pleasures, passing our days in malice and envy, hated by others and hating one another" (Titus 3:3). This should drive each of us "not to think of himself more highly than he ought to think, but to think with sober judgment, each according to the measure of faith that God has assigned" (Rom. 12:3). The end result will be an ability to look at biblical texts with different eyes. And this is an essential element of expository apologetics.

(4) We must not avoid the tough questions. The apostle Paul gives us three very clear examples of this practice in the book of Romans. We find his first rhetorical question in chapter 6: "What shall we say then? Are we to continue in sin that grace may abound? By no means! How can we who died to sin still live in it?" (vv. 1–2).

His second question is in chapter 9: "What shall we say then? Is there injustice on God's part? By no means! For he says to Moses, 'I will have mercy on whom I have mercy, and I will have compassion on whom I have compassion'" (vv. 14–15).

And finally, toward the end of chapter 9 he asks, "What shall we say, then? That Gentiles who did not pursue righteousness have attained it, that is, a righteousness that is by faith; but that Israel who pursued a law that would lead to righteousness did not succeed in reaching that law" (vv. 30–31).

In each case, the apostle is tackling the tough questions related to his teaching. He has heard these questions countless times and knows that he will hear them again. They are questions that honest skeptics have asked, and he has decided to incorporate them into his teaching ministry. Nor are they the easiest questions he faced. These are difficult. In fact, they remain among the most difficult questions that people who teach Pauline doctrine face, and if we are to engage in expository apologetics, we should follow the apostle's lead and refuse to avoid difficult questions.

Face-to-Face Objections

Another thing we learn from the aforementioned apostolic example is the importance of face-to-face apologetics. Paul's rhetorical questions came from his interactions with unbelievers. This is what separates the deft apologist from the clumsy beginner.

I once met a former professional fighter who was training an up-and-coming contender. Speaking about his young protégé's progress, the trainer said, "I could probably beat him right now, but in another six months, I wouldn't have a chance." What he was referring to was not the fact that the young fighter was becoming bigger and stronger, but that he was becoming wiser. He was seeing combinations and becoming more comfortable with them. He was beginning to anticipate and counter more effectively. Soon, he would be so fluid in his recognition and response that his youth, strength, and stamina would overwhelm the older fighter.

This is a perfect picture of what happens to us as we engage in the battle of apologetics (Jude 3).[1] As we interact with skeptics, we hear objections again and again. After a while, we become comfortable answering them. Eventually, we begin to anticipate them. However, this does not happen unless we engage. We have to get outside of our bubbles and interact with real people who have real questions.

Objections from Friends and Family

Objections from friends and family members can be a particularly useful resource for the expository apologist. The doubts, questions, and objections of the people closest to you may at times cause frustration.

However, they can provide you with perspectives that will stretch you in helpful ways. Don't be afraid to get your hands dirty in the lives of lost people. Of course, for some of us, this may take some effort.

In July 2012, I entered the fascinating world of martial arts. I grew up playing ball—any kind of ball. Whatever sport was in season, that's the one I was playing. I never took karate, tae kwon do, or anything like it. That just wasn't of interest to me. Nor was I interested in starting now. Especially if I had to enter some dojo and start digesting Eastern mysticism. Then I found Brazilian Jiu Jitsu. To make a long story short, my oldest son wanted to train; I am always looking for things we can do together—voila! Eventually, he went another direction, but it was too late for me; I was hooked.

I love the art itself. It is the most practical, effective self-defense-based martial art on the planet. There is no striking involved, no Eastern mysticism, no Cobra Kai hopped up on soda pop and jolly ranchers—just my speed. I experience the discipline, camaraderie, physical and mental challenge, and accountability I missed from my sports days. I also found an outlet for my desire to compete. To date, I've competed in numerous tournaments, won a number of titles (including a gold medal at the Pan American Championships in 2014), and look forward to more. More importantly, Jiu Jitsu provides me with two days a week building relationships with nonchurch folks in the real world. For a pastor, that's like an oasis in the middle of a desert!

I love the church. However, for pastors, it is very easy to become ghettoized. We spend our time preparing sermons, counseling, visiting, comforting, marrying, burying, and fellowshipping. Decades can pass with no opportunity to navigate the obstacles inherent to relationships with people who can't understand the Word, let alone sign off on your statement of faith. The result can be an approach to reading, studying, and teaching the Bible in a sterile, compartmentalized manner. We all need those relationships in our lives that make us ask, "Now what would Jimmy say if I read this text to him?"

Objections from Evangelistic Encounters

At its core, expository apologetics is merely a tool in the toolbox of the personal evangelist. Apologetics is not an end in itself; it is a means to an end. Our goal is the gospel. It does us no good to answer objections for objections' sake. We answer objections and questions in order to remove obstacles that obscure people's view of the gospel. And that gospel is "the power of God unto salvation" (Rom. 1:16). We are not out to win arguments; our goal is to win souls. As the proverbs teach, "Whoever wins souls is wise" (Prov. 11:30).

If this is not your desire, then I encourage you to rethink your objective. If you merely want to win a few arguments and "put people in their place" when they disagree with you, you've missed the point:

> And Jesus came and said to them, "All authority in heaven and on earth has been given to me. Go therefore and make disciples of all nations, baptizing them in the name of the Father and of the Son and of the Holy Spirit, teaching them to observe all that I have commanded you. And behold, I am with you always, to the end of the age." (Matt. 28:18–20)

This is our commission! And it is inherently evangelistic. We are called to make disciples. This involves taking the gospel to all the world. As we do, we "baptize them in the name of the Father and of the Son and of the Holy Spirit." We don't simply walk into various cultures and ask, "Would you like to be baptized today?" This is a byproduct of evangelism. People hear the gospel, they are converted, then they are baptized.

This is the pattern we see in the Acts of the Apostles. It is what happened with the crowd converted under Peter's preaching at Pentecost (Acts 2:41), the Ethiopian eunuch (8:36), the apostle Paul (9:18), Cornelius and his household (10:48), Lydia and her household (16:14–15), the Philippian jailer and his household (16:32), "many of the Corinthians hearing Paul" (18:8), and the disciples in Ephesus (19:5). This is the evangelistic pattern of our Great Commission.

Nor is this exclusively the province of the apostles. We have all been given this same commission:

> All this is from God, who through Christ reconciled us to himself and gave us the ministry of reconciliation; that is, in Christ God was reconciling the world to himself, not counting their trespasses against them, and entrusting to us the message of reconciliation.

Therefore, we are ambassadors for Christ, God making his appeal through us. We implore you on behalf of Christ, be reconciled to God. (2 Cor. 5:18–20)

We are "ambassadors for Christ." As ambassadors, it is our privilege to represent our King in a foreign land. "And this gospel of the kingdom will be proclaimed throughout the whole world as a testimony to all nations, and then the end will come" (Matt. 24:14).

Objections from the Encounters of Frontline Evangelists Who Need Our Help

Two types of people find themselves on the front lines of evangelistic encounters regularly. First, we see the Matthews among us. These are people who have come to Christ and still have significant friendships, in both number and strategic importance. Like Matthew in the New Testament, these believers take advantage of tremendous opportunities to leverage their influence and relationships to bring people into gospel encounters (see Luke 5:29–32).

The second group are the Pauls among us. These people, unlike the Matthews, do not have strategic relationships simply as a result of their situation in life; they create strategic opportunities as a way of life. A person in this group was not necessarily popular before his conversion; he might not have a significant number of friends (and usually an accompanying short window of opportunity). This is the guy who rolls out of bed in the morning and ends up in conversations the rest of us only dream about—or hear about from people like them!

In both cases, the expository apologist seeking to think strategically about how to apply his approach to the way he preaches and teaches has a simple task—make yourself available as a resource for those on the front lines. Doing so will result in at least three significant advantages.

First, you will contribute to the advance of the gospel through those frontline evangelists. Whether a person is a Matthew or a Paul, his opportunity, availability, and zeal must be paired with knowledge and skill. It is one thing to have an opportunity to be in front of lost people. It is quite a different thing to know what to say and how to say it.

Having lunch with the newly converted college student, businessman, or police officer will help him gain important knowledge about sharing the gospel in his sphere of influence. This is a crucial component of discipleship.

Second, you will gain a better understanding of the questions and patterns of objections people encounter in the world. As you engage with the Matthews and Pauls in your life, you will begin to hear the same questions again and again. This in turn will give you both insight and confidence. You will have your finger on the pulse of frontline encounters, and you will come to realize that the questions are not as complex as you thought, nor are the answers as elusive as you imagined.

Third, you will have to engage in expository apologetics on a personal level, which will contribute to your ability to do so on a corporate level. As you go through the process of fielding and answering questions in an effort to help others, you will develop your apologetic chops. Everything you do on a personal level will translate into more effective reading of texts and audiences analysis, which in turn will result in more effective expository apologetics in your preaching or teaching.

BROADER CULTURAL OBJECTIONS

In addition to personal, face-to-face objections, a second category of objections arises from the broader culture. As information becomes more readily available, our world becomes smaller. The result is a gold mine of information concerning the objections our culture has concerning the gospel we preach.

The news and social media are important sources of popular objections. News is driven by ratings, and ratings, in the news media, are driven by what people want to know. Social media, on the other hand, is a living, breathing data mine where reactions are immediate and usually unfiltered.

The News

I should clarify that the news is not purely ratings driven. The media do operate from a genuine bias, which leads to overemphasizing some aspects of stories and de-emphasizing other aspects. A classic example is the Kermit Gosnell story. Gosnell is the Philadelphia-based ob-gyn who ran an abortion mill where he routinely killed babies who survived abortions. The story is notorious, not only because of what the doctor did but also because the news media all but ignored it due to the negative light it shone on abortion.

This does not mean that we have nothing to learn from the news. The fact that the news media is biased is in fact a clue as to their objections to the Christian worldview. We can learn as much from what they choose not to cover as we can from what they overemphasize. Instead of rejecting the news because we disagree with what they choose to cover, the expository apologist asks, "Why are there so many stories about X when Y seems so much more important?" The answer leads us right where we want to go—to the major objections in the news.

As a pastor, it is important not only to help people think about expository apologetic issues; it is also important to help them see where they come from. It can be helpful for those who listen to us to have someone point out to them the fact that the things they see on the news are presented in a manner designed not merely to inform, but to shape their thinking.

Social Media

Full disclosure: I am not a fan of social media. I see it as a necessary evil. Facebook, Twitter, LinkedIn, YouTube, and the rest are black holes where one can lose untold hours of actual productivity, deceive oneself into viewing cyber relationships as an acceptable substitute for real ones, forget the rules of basic civility, and obliterate one's Christian witness in the process. And that's just the short list!

However, having said all that, social media is here to stay. It is the Mars Hill/Areopagus of our day. It is the place where many people "spend their time in nothing except telling or hearing something new" (Acts 17:21). As such, it is a great place to practice expository apologetics, and to become aware of the current objections gaining a hearing in the culture at large.

For example, I have been working on a rebuttal to the civil rights line of argumentation currently dominating the same-sex "marriage" debate. In doing so, I have used Facebook and Twitter as a testing ground of sorts. Sometimes I will post a link to an article or video on the topic of same-sex "marriage" with a few words making my position clear. Within minutes I will have dozens—sometimes hundreds—of responses. Most of the responses will be consistent with the biblical position. But there are always those who disagree, and are eager to make it known. Consequently, I have seen a clear pattern in the way people are thinking and arguing about this topic. That, in turn, has helped me sharpen my apologetic and my pastoral ministry.

As a pastor, it is beneficial to have real-time, real-life examples of the arguments that have gained popularity in the culture at large. If I see something repeated on Facebook and Twitter, it is likely that the people whom God has called me to lead are hearing the same thing on the job, at school, or in their dealings with family and friends. As such, it is incumbent upon me to provide them with ways of thinking about and responding to these issues.

This also applies to my role as a father. My children are growing up in a world dominated by social media. And although I try to keep them away from it as long as I can, they are still affected by the overflow. They know what's going on in the world. They hear the same arguments I encounter when I post controversial stories. As their father, it is my duty to prepare them to think through and respond to such arguments. In fact, it is not at all unusual for there to be robust discussions around our dinner table concerning the latest argument I encountered on Twitter.

OBJECTIONS IN THE ACADEMY

While the news and social media give us insight into what popular culture is thinking, the academy sheds light on those individuals who are shaping the thinking of others. Most of the ideas that have gained popularity today started out as theories in the academy a generation or so ago. And, due to the speed and ease with which information travels these days, that process has been condensed considerably. Hence, instead of taking a generation to affect the thinking of the masses, today's academy can do it in a matter of days or weeks. Three examples stand out in this regard: the new atheists, the Jesus Seminar, and the New Perspective on Paul.

The new atheists may have declined in popularity. However, they have not gone away. Their new breed of skepticism touched a nerve in a broad cross section of society. Unlike their predecessors, the new atheists are not limited to success in the academic arena. Christopher Hitchens is a household name. Moreover, their virulent anti-Christian rhetoric has been given a pass in the press. As a preacher, one cannot address, for example, passages involving warfare and the "slaying of the wicked" without the new elephant in the room: "What about those people who say this is why religion is evil?"

The Jesus Seminar is less popular than the new atheists. However, they represent the baseline of contemporary opposition to the gospel. People may not know Marcus Borg and John Dominic Crossan by name, but they are probably aware of the *Search for the Historical Jesus* and all it entails. For a while, back in the 1980s and '90s, the Jesus Seminar was regular fare on the *History* channel and in magazines like *Time* and *Newsweek*. Their skepticism was front-page news every Christmas and Easter.

The people to whom we preach are more aware of the work of this group than they know or care to admit. Whenever you read a passage of Scripture touching on the virgin birth, death, resurrection, or even the teaching of Jesus, questions arise: "Did that really happen?" or, "Did Jesus really say that, or was it added by the later Christian community in an effort to deify Christ?" As expository apologists, we must always be ready to give an answer to the one who questions the very assumption that we can trust the Bible from which we preach.

The New Perspective on Paul is a more recent phenomenon with much more far-reaching implications. Whereas the new atheists are obvious outsiders, and the Jesus Seminar represents obvious apostasy, the New Perspective movement is more mainstream. This movement comes from a camp that upholds and affirms the historicity of the Bible. And its main exponent, N. T. Wright, is an intelligent, articulate, winsome theologian—with a British accent to boot!

At its core, the New Perspective movement is about the doctrine of justification and whether the "traditional" Pauline reading/understanding is valid.

Classical/Historical Objections

When contemplating major issues in apologetics, we must remember Solomon's words in Ecclesiastes: "What has been is what will be, and what has been done is what will be done, and there is nothing new under the sun. Is there a thing of which it is said, 'See, this is new'? It has been already in the ages before us" (Eccles. 1:9–10). This is absolutely the case with apologetics. However, recent history provides a number of new twists on old objections.

The Reformation

Solomon's words in Ecclesiastes 1:9 are as true today as ever. One need only be slightly familiar with church history to realize that everything we are seeing today in terms of apostasy, heresy, heterodoxy, fads, and trends has already been done before . . . and much better, at that!

The Reformation was a time of intense debate and dialogue over key theological issues. Questions such as, "What is the Bible?" and "How are men saved?" took center stage as the greatest minds of the day preached sermons, wrote pamphlets and books, and penned confessions to clarify their positions. The result is a rich heritage of theological discourse that will serve the expository apologist well.

Major Debates throughout History

The history of the church is riddled with theological debates and disagreements. For example, the early Roman Empire was a hotbed of such debates. As James Robertson notes:

> We might expect to find that, when the persecutions by the heathen were at an end within the Roman empire, Christians lived together in peace and love, according to their Lord's commandment; but it is a sad truth that they now began to be very much divided by quarrels among themselves. There had, indeed, been many false teachers in earlier times; but now, when the emperor had become a Christian, the troubles caused by such persons reached much further than before. The emperors took part in them, and made laws about them, and the whole empire was stirred by them.[2]

Once there was political power to be had by those who professed Christ, the floodgates were opened for the entrance of heretics and false professors. In response, the faithful had to rise to the occasion and fight back the wolves. This resulted in a series of major debates.

These debates and others throughout the years are another great source of objections for the expository apologist. They are helpful in at least three ways. First, these debates give us insight into the thoughts of those who object to our message. It is one thing to encounter a quasi-intellectual who has heard an objection or two to Christianity and enjoys spouting them off in an attempt to stump his Christian friends. It is a different thing altogether to read cogent, well-thought-out, high-level objections from men who have devoted a great deal of thought and study to the matters about which they speak.

Second, in addition to helping us understand how skeptics think, major debates offer us a treasure trove of sound biblical thinking that has stood the test of time. Augustine vs. Pelagius, Luther vs. Erasmus, Calvin vs. Arminius. We have at our fingertips not only the original records of the debates, but also material from the centuries after. Jonathan Edwards's *Freedom of the Will*, for example, is a direct result of Luther's work, *The Bondage of the Will,* which he wrote in response to his debates with Erasmus. And who can count the number of books stemming from the Calvin/Arminius debate?

Finally, these debates affirm our contention that there are only a limited number of objections, and all of them answerable. Cracking the pages of a book like *The Bondage of the Will* is an exercise in faith-building. At its core, this work, and others like it, serves to remind us that (1) the Bible is worthy of careful reading and study; (2) the doctrines expounded therein are boundless in their depth and beauty; (3) even the most astute opponent is no match for the truth God has revealed; and (4) we are not alone in this fight.

Biblical Objections

In addition to the debates and arguments throughout the history of the church, the Bible itself is a source of objections and answers. We have already examined several examples of this. However, it is worth noting again that the biblical authors answered direct objections from their opponents. Here again, the apostle Paul—the original expository apologist—will serve as our example:

Now if Christ is proclaimed as raised from the dead, how can some of you say that there is no resurrection of the dead? But if there is no resurrection of the dead, then not even Christ has been raised. And if Christ has not been raised, then our preaching is in vain and your faith is in vain. We are even found to be misrepresenting God, because we testified about God that he raised Christ, whom he did not raise if it is true that the dead are not raised. For if the dead are not raised, not even Christ has been raised. And if Christ has not been raised, your faith is futile and you are still in your sins. Then those also who have fallen asleep in Christ have perished. If in Christ we have hope in this life only, we are of all people most to be pitied. (1 Cor. 15:12–19)

Notice that Paul identifies the objection ("some of you say that there is no resurrection of the dead"), then proceeds to offer several logical consequences to such thinking. All of the consequences he mentions are related directly to the gospel he preached and its implications.

Nor is Paul alone in countering objections. John addressed the Gnostic heresy in 1 John. Peter addressed the historicity of the gospel in his first epistle. Jude addressed christological heresy. And this is just the tip of the iceberg! The New Testament is replete with answers to objections—objections that have not changed and will not change since "the hope that is in us" is based on that unchanging revelation.

As preachers and teachers, we must rely on this wealth of information as we develop our expository apologetics. Being aware and informed of the objections in our surroundings, in history, and in the Bible will aid us in our preaching and teaching. When studying a text, we can ask ourselves, "When has this text been challenged?" and "What are the doctrines addressed herein that have been debated in the past?"

I'm not talking about an extended excursion every week. This is not about adding a research project to what you're already doing. This is something that will happen over time. As you begin to think like an expository apologist, you will automatically begin to approach Scripture in this way. Usually, this will result in nothing more than an acknowledgment of and response to the questions people are likely to ask in response to your message. However, at times you will tap into something more. Over time, since there is nothing new under the sun, you will eventually be able to reference these things naturally and without much additional work. Providentially, that will also be the time when you discover that you are much more fluent in your discussions with strangers, and much more willing to engage at any time.

DISCIPLE MAKING AND EXPOSITORY APOLOGETICS

Not all of us are preachers or teachers. Nor should we be (James 3:1). However, we are all called to make disciples. As we have already seen, this disciple-making task is linked inexorably to our approach to expository apologetics. However, in order to understand just how this works, we need to back up a bit and look at discipleship as a whole.

Three Approaches to Discipleship

When we say the word *discipleship*, people generally think about one of two scenarios. I call them the "assembly line" approach and the "kung fu" approach. The assembly line approach is based on the idea that discipleship is a step in the process of getting Christians from point A to point B in the process of "plugging them in" to our church or ministry. In this approach, discipleship consists of a class or series of classes in which we cover the "basics" of Christianity. This usually includes things like "How to Know You're a Christian"; "How to Have a Quiet Time"; "How to Share Your Faith"; "Finding Your Spiritual Gifts"; and "How to Go Deeper."

The kung fu approach is based on the idea of "shared life" and mentoring. When I say "kung fu," I'm not referring to the martial art, but the TV series I watched as a kid. In the series, the main character, Caine, wandered through the Old West seeking a peaceful existence, but never able to find it (he had to fight at least once in each episode). The series used a flashback technique to take you to the time when Cain was a boy being trained by his wise, old, blind master. The idea of the show was that Cain was prepared for every encounter he had as a man by the "discipleship" of his master when he was a boy.

The kung fu approach to discipleship is not about a series of lessons. As the proponents of this approach will tell you, "It's not about information; it's about relationships." Of course, the Christian version of this approach to discipleship is more about "hanging out" than it is about the deliberate training and preparation of a disciple. Nevertheless, this is a common approach to discipleship.

Each of these approaches contains a kernel of truth. However, they are both deficient. In the first instance, it is true that disciple making is about passing on a set of basic, fundamental truths. However, the way the assembly line approach has developed in recent years is purely pragmatic and utilitarian. The idea is that people need to be made fit for their "place in the machine." On the other hand, the kung fu approach is absolutely correct in insisting on relationship over time as a key component of discipleship. However, in its modern expression, there is almost no emphasis on passing on information in a formal, structured way.

The expository apologetic model is in some ways a combination of these. The emphasis, as we saw in chapter 5, is on connecting disciples to a specific body of information. This information is not about making people cogs in a machine; it is about connecting them to historic Christianity in a meaningful, memorable way. There is a body of information, in the form of creeds, confessions, and catechisms, that disciples need to know. This is the essence of the Great Commission (Matt. 28:18–20). Making disciples is about "teaching them to observe all that I have commanded you" (28:20). The goal is not for people to see me (the disciple maker) as the master, but for them to see Christ.

Nor is this done over the course of a few classes. Catechesis takes years! As a parent, my goal is to catechize my children daily and to develop a habit in them that will last a lifetime. The body of knowledge we are passing on is far too significant to be covered in a few weeks. Knowing this changes the way we view the disciple-making process. It also puts us on a course that makes expository apologetics natural.

As we walk through life with those whom we disciple, we will find ourselves using the creeds, catechisms, and confessions as discipleship tools. As issues and questions arise, we will go back again and again to the things we have asked them to memorize and make the connection between rote memory and real life. This process of going from information to application is the essence of discipleship. And it is not merely informational. We grow as we walk through life together. In doing so, we use many of the means mentioned above in relation to preaching and teaching. However, the context is different. Instead of referencing an article, book, current event, or sermon (as we would in a sermon), we can actually sit down and walk through the material together. In doing so, we go beyond merely engaging in expository apologetics to actually making an expository apologist.

CONCLUSION

Whether you are preparing a sermon for a congregation, developing a lesson for a small group, gearing up to lead family worship, or just trying to "always be ready" when the opportunity arises, your expository apologetics journey begins with having an awareness of objections. If we are not aware of objections, we will never seek to answer them. We will merely assume that everybody is on board with what we say. Of course, this is not the case, and when objections come, we are often caught flatfooted. On the other hand, if we are constantly aware of objections, we will always be ready.

Remember, the goal here is not to be consumed with the objections that are out there. On the contrary, our emphasis is on the truth to which people object. Our goal is to grow deeper in our understanding of and commitment to the gospel. In the process we become aware of the objections people have to it. If we start with objections, we begin an endless spiral that will consume our time and energy and move us away from our life of devotion to Christ. However, starting with the gospel drives us deeper in our devotion. Our goal is God! The objections we face are obstacles to be removed, not distractions to pursue. Keep this in mind, and you will be well on your way to being an effective expository apologist.

Appendix

Example of an Expository Apologetic Sermon

The following sermon was given on February 6, 2015, as part of Moody's Founder's Week.

This area and issue of cultural apologetics is one that has been near and dear to my heart for a long time, and as a person who thinks about things from this perspective and looks at what's going on around us from the perspective of cultural apologetics, there are a number of things that are just unavoidable. Chief among them is the issue of homosexuality and so-called "same-sex marriage."

And not only is this a raging issue within our culture, but it is also an issue that has crept into the church in ways that are surprising to many. And one of the things that's most surprising is the way that people in your generation, speaking about college students and people in their twenties and thirties, people in your generation have capitulated on the issue of homosexuality. It amazes me when I talk to twenty-somethings and thirty-somethings how you have in many ways sort of changed your thinking so that homosexuality now is not the sin or the problem; the problem is the church and the way the church treats homosexuals. I'm always taken aback when I hear that, but it's pretty universal. It's pretty universal, this idea that the problem is us. Because, if we were just nicer, then this issue wouldn't be what this issue is. That is not only naive; it's dangerous, and it borders on heretical. It borders on heretical—for a number of reasons.

Number 1, because it blames the beautiful, glorious bride of Christ for sin and degradation. And secondly, because it unwittingly accepts the idea of justification by niceness. There is an eleventh commandment, and the eleventh commandment is "Thou shalt be nice." And we do not believe in the first ten. So speaking on this issue usually results in people saying something like, "Well, what you said might have been true, but the way that you said it just wasn't nice. And therefore, I just can't get on board with you."

So, wait a minute. Let me see if I understand this correctly. I just talked about sin and abomination and you were not upset nearly as much by that sin and that abomination as you are by the fact that I wasn't "nice." And so because of that, you are willing to judge me for my judgment, but not judge them for what God says is an abomination. Am I understanding that accurately? And the answer to the question is yes, that's exactly what's happening. That is precisely what's happening.

And because of it, this movement is rolling like a steam roller, and it's coming after the church. Don't you believe for a moment that we can continue to move in the direction that we're moving and allow the church to continue to be the church. Because if homosexuality is successfully normalized, as it has been, and if "same-sex marriage" is understood to be legal and put on par with ethnicity, then that means it is no more correct to allow the church to discriminate in that area than it would be to allow the church to discriminate on ethnicity. Which means we *will* conform or die, from their perspective.

Know this. We cannot be left alone. Because if the other side is right, we must cease to exist. If the other side is right, being marginalized is not enough. We must be destroyed, in the sense that Christianity as we know it must be gutted of every last fiber of its foundational and fundamental understandings. That's the only way that this thing goes. And there are young people in this room who are part of that undermining effort without even knowing it.

And then there's a second layer of this. And that second layer of this is people who are part of that undermining effort out of ignorance. And I want to deal with that, more so, today. Because one of the chief arguments that is being used today is this argument: Why do you pick and choose?

Most Christians can't answer that question. You go to Leviticus and you talk about the abomination of homosexuality but you eat shrimp. You wear clothes of blended material. You shave the edges of your beard. So why, dear Christian, do you pick and choose?

Most Christians respond to that question with, "Well, I . . . because I . . . I . . . that's just . . . I never noticed that clock up there before. I, uh, that's an amazing piece of digital machinery, that thing right there." We have no idea. We have no idea where to even start answering that question. And so because of that, it is being emphasized more and more and more.

There's a famous episode of the TV show *The West Wing* where the president is dealing with a woman who is a radio talk show host and it's supposed to represent—and I won't even tell you who it's supposed to represent, but there's a female talk show host and the president just takes her to task. And he comes and there's something happening there in the White House, you know, she's there and he just attacks her and just rips her to shreds. I just want to know, you called it an abomination, and I just want to know. Do we need to stone the Redskins for playing football with a dead pig? How 'bout my this? How 'bout my that? And he just goes on this whole litany. Basically, the smackdown is all about this question: Why do you get to pick and choose?

We have to answer that question. We have to. Peter makes it clear that we are to always be ready to give an answer to anyone who asks us the reason for the hope that is in us. We have to do that. So, we have to answer.

So, how do we answer? I'll tell you how I answer that question. The first thing I do is, I acknowledge the fact that I pick and choose. But I know *why* I pick and choose. Why is this important? Because the person who's accusing me also picks and chooses, but they don't know why.

So open with me if you would to Leviticus. We'll look first at Leviticus 18 and the accusation against me and those who hold the position that I do. Leviticus 18, beginning at 22, "You shall not lie with a male as with a woman; it is an abomination. And you shall not lie with any animal and so make yourself unclean with it, neither shall any woman give herself to an animal to lie with it: it is a perversion." There it is. And we go there, and they say, "OK, OK, fine. That's there, granted.

But you pick and choose because of all the things that I said before—you eat shrimp, you cut your beard, you do all of these other sort of things." And we just go abbabbabbba.

First thing I do is I say, "Yup, I pick and choose. I absolutely pick and choose. I cut my beard, yup, I do, you know, the whole shrimp thing. I love me some shrimp. Love me some shrimp. In fact, it's best when it's wrapped with bacon." Amen, hallelujah, praise the Lord.

But you also pick and choose. And so you go forward, for example chapter 19. Look at 19 verse 11: "You shall not steal; you shall not deal falsely; you shall not lie to one another." Guess what. The person who's accusing me of choosing hypocritically wants to obey that law, but not the ones around it. Which means *they* pick and choose hypocritically.

There's more. Look at verse 13: "You shall not oppress your neighbor or rob him. The wages of a hired worker shall not remain with you all night until the morning. You shall not curse the deaf or put a stumbling block before the blind. You shall fear your God. I am the LORD." Go on, next paragraph. "You shall do no injustice in court." I mean, we can go on and on and on. Right here in this Levitical code. And these people who point the finger and say, "You're a hypocrite because you uphold this part of Leviticus and not that part of Leviticus" do the same thing. But what's the difference between us and them, those of us who are informed on this issue? The difference is, we have reason to do so, and they do not.

What is the reason that I do so? Well, there are a number of reasons that I do so. Let me give them to you, in turn.

Number 1, I do so, and let me just say this up front: My answer is based on my understanding of the Scriptures as a Reformed Baptist. I stand in the historic tradition of Protestant Reformed thinking on this issue. There are others who may come at this a slightly different way than I do, but the point is still the same. We have reason to do what we do.

So, number 1: I do this because I understand the threefold division of the law. I do this because I understand the threefold division of the law, that not all laws are the same. I understand that there are moral laws that are forever binding on all people in all places, and that there are ceremonial laws, and that those ceremonial laws prefigured Christ and his work and had to do with the worship of Israel, which is the reason that we understand the work of Christ. And then there are civil laws, and that these civil laws, were specifically for the nation of Israel as a nation.

Listen to the way it's expressed in this historic Baptist confession, the Second London Baptist Confession of 1689—so this is not new thinking, OK? This is Second London, it's also Westminster. So, again, listen to this. All the historic Protestant Reformed confessions will give you this threefold division of the law.

On the chapter "Of the Law," paragraph 2: "The same law," talking about this moral law, "that was first written in the heart of man continued to be a perfect rule of righteousness after the fall, and was delivered by God onto Mount Sinai, in Ten Commandments, and written in two tablets, the four first containing our duty toward God, and the other six, our duty to man." So the moral law, summarized in the Ten Commandments, that the confession goes on to say binds all people everywhere.

Paragraph 3: "Besides this law, commonly called moral, God was pleased to give to the people of Israel ceremonial laws, containing several typical ordinances, partly of worship, prefiguring Christ, his graces, action, sufferings, and benefits; and partly holding forth divers instructions of moral duties, all which ceremonial laws being appointed only to the time of reformation, are by Jesus Christ the true Messiah and only law-giver, who was furnished with power from the Father, for that end abrogated and taken away."

We're not obligated to keep the ceremonial law. They pointed to Christ and his finished work. It's done. Amen? It's done. So I don't have to go slay animals. The Lamb has been slain. But I wouldn't have understood *the* Lamb that was slain without the ceremonial system where lambs were slain. I wouldn't understand *the* Passover and Christ as the Passover Lamb were it not for Israel keeping the Passover for thousands of years so that when Christ came and the picture was brought to fruition, I could understand what God was communicating. That's my relationship with the ceremonial law.

Four: "To them also he gave sundry judicial laws, which expired together with the state of that people, not obliging any now by virtue of that institution; their general equity only being of moral use." Israel had certain laws that were civil laws, that were particular for Israel in the ancient Near East, and are not particular for us, because we don't live in Israel in the ancient Near East.

Folks, this historic understanding answers an abundance of questions in terms of why we pick and choose when we go to the law. If you understand that there is moral law, there is ceremonial law, and that there is civil law, it makes all the sense in the world that there would be some things that you would hold to and obey, and other things that you wouldn't. You have an example of some of that here, back in Leviticus 18. If you begin—Leviticus 18 starts there in verse 6 with the moral teaching about incest. After you have the moral teaching about incest, you have the moral teaching about homosexuality, and after that you have the moral teaching about bestiality. This is based on the moral law. This is based on the Ten Commandments. "You shall not commit adultery." That moral law is foundational to this. So that we understand that these are moral teachings.

Here's an example of that: There are a lot of people who are arguing today, one judge for example, in Australia, is arguing that laws on the books against incest ought to be overturned. Why? Because we have two things that make it no longer necessary. Number 1, we have genetic testing, and two, we have abortion. Since we have genetic testing and abortion, and the only reason to have laws against incest is because of genetic maladies that it may cause with children, then we no longer need this law. If we had time, we could read through this first section here and we could see, for example, that the incest laws cover more than blood relatives. God doesn't give the incest laws solely because of the things that can happen to a child who is born of incest. The incest laws have to do with morality and the way that relations are to be held. Not because of possible consequences. It's based on the moral law.

Then we could go forward, for example, to look at chapter 19, beginning in verse 5: "When you offer a sacrifice of peace offerings to the LORD, you shall offer it so that you may be accepted." That's obviously ceremonial. Amen? So immediately I know that I'm not going to go and rip that right out of its context and take it and apply it right here to my situation and circumstance. I need to read that through the lens of the purpose of the ceremony. It is only then that I can understand how this law is applicable.

So the first answer to that question, why do I pick and choose? First answer is, you pick and choose too. Don't forget answer number 1. We all pick and choose. And that's powerful, folks. Because here's what people are doing, when they do that. They're standing on their moral high horse, looking down at you: "You narrow-minded, bigoted, unkind, so-called Christian. How dare you. All the stuff in the Bible that you overlook. You do this and you do that, yet you have the audacity to hold on to this antiquated rule about homosexuality." That's what they're saying. So immediately when you go, "Yeah, you know I do, you're right, I do. You do too. Just come on down here. Let's get right here, all right. You do too." "No, I don't." Yes, you do. Here's a couple of things right here that come out of the same part of the law. I can't believe you, you hypocrite. But it's OK, we're hypocrites together. All right? We're hypocrites together. Why am I smiling and acknowledging that I'm a hypocrite? Because I know somebody who saves hypocrites. Amen?

Second answer is the threefold division of the law. The third answer? Progressive revelation. This is not all we have. Amen, somebody! 'Cause that's good news, right there. If all we had was Leviticus, Lord help you today! But this is not all we have. So if I'm going to interpret these laws, I have to interpret them in light of the rest of what God has revealed. As Paul Harvey would say, "The rest of the story."

So, go forward, turn to the right, and look for example in the book of Matthew. Look in Matthew. Matthew chapter 5, verse 1: "Seeing the crowds, he went up on the mountain, and when he sat down, his disciples came to him. And he opened his mouth and taught them."

Now, just briefly, if I can take a moment here, let me put this in its context. Matthew is writing this Gospel, he's writing this Gospel for a Jewish audience. He wants his Jewish audience to know one thing and one thing only. Jesus is the one for whom we've been waiting. So he starts off in chapter 1 with one of those things that we really don't like to read, a genealogy. We don't like them. Go on, tell the truth, shame the Devil, you don't like them. You don't like the genealogies. You get to the genealogy and it's this person, that person, you can't pronounce the names, whatever. But in this genealogy, Matthew is pointing back to something. Genesis chapter 3 in verse 15, there is a promise made after the fall. The promise is made in the form of the curse to the Serpent. "I will put enmity between you and the woman, and between your seed and her seed; he shall bruise you on the head, and you shall bruise him on the heel" (NASB). So there is one who is coming who is the seed of the woman from this particular line who is going to crush the head of the Serpent. From then on, the rest of the Bible is about the protection and preservation and coming of this promised seed. We get to Matthew, and in chapter 1 Matthew says, "Jesus is the promised seed."

Then you get to chapter 2. And in chapter 2 there's the visit of the wise men and then there's Herod. Now, Herod wants to do something we've seen before. Herod wants to kill the male children of Israel. We saw that before. Now, the promised seed was in Genesis; the protected seed was protected from Pharaoh in Exodus. So now we've gone from Genesis and the promised seed to Exodus and the protected seed. That's who Jesus is. He then goes to Egypt in order to fulfill the prophecy, "Out of Egypt I have called my son." Just like Israel went to Egypt and then was called out of Egypt.

Now we come to chapter 3. And in chapter 3, he's baptized, just like Israel was in coming through the Jordan. Then we come to chapter 4, and all of a sudden in chapter 4, he's tempted. Not just any old kind of way. Lust of the eyes, lust of the flesh, boastful pride of life—just like the first Adam was tempted. So now we have Jesus as the promised seed, Jesus as protected seed, Jesus as faithful Israel brought up out of Egypt. Now we have Jesus as the baptized one coming into the land of promise, and we have Jesus as the last Adam who succeeds where the first Adam fails.

Now in chapter 5 he goes up on a mountain and starts teaching. He's the true lawgiver. And he says things like, "You have heard it said . . . but I say unto you." So now Jesus becomes our interpretive key for going back to and understanding the law that was given by Moses. So in essence he's the greater Moses. So now, I not only have the threefold division of the law, which helps me pick and choose with integrity in the Old Testament, but I also have progressive revelation, so that Jesus now comes and helps me understand how it is that I am to see the law in light of his coming. So no, I'm not being arbitrary.

There's a third answer. And this third answer is very important. Because if all I do is just give somebody an answer and make them feel bad about asking me that question, I can go away and be somewhat delighted. I'm just gonna go on and tell the truth. I can go on and be happy. God's still working on me. Amen? But that's not enough. I don't just want to be right in this debate. My dog in this fight is not about what I like to see in the culture. My dog in this fight is not about me wanting to control other people's lives. My dog in this fight is this: the Bible tells me that marriage between a man and a woman is a picture of the covenant relationship between Jesus Christ and his bride the church, so that anything other than that is blaspheming Christ and his gospel. That's why I have a dog in this fight.

And so that last place that we go is this. Number 1: I pick and choose, you pick and choose too. Number 2: I pick and choose based on the threefold division of the law. Number 3: I have to pick and choose because of progressive revelation. It wouldn't make sense *not* to pick and choose because of progressive revelation. Number 4: I pick and choose because the law is not an end in itself. This is the other thing because the law is meant to point us to something greater, because the law is meant to show us that we are all sinners and hypocrites, that's why we get right here. Not because, "Oh, you're no better than me." No, we need to get right here because ultimately what I want to tell you is that, yes, I'm a hypocrite, but, yes, so are you. Ultimately what I want to tell you is that you pick and choose, and I'm worried about you because you don't have a legitimate reason to pick and choose. Yes, I'm worried about you, because you think you are all right with God, and I want you to know, I'm not, apart from the person and work of Jesus Christ! And the law is what helps me to see and understand that. Not the eleventh commandment. We know from Galatians, "By the works of the law shall no flesh be justified." We understand that there are none righteous, no not even one! We understand that all we like sheep have gone astray, each one of us has turned to his own way, but God hath laid upon him the iniquity of us all.

Why is it important for me to understand sin? It's important for me to understand sin because if I don't understand sin, I don't understand my need for a Savior. So you see, I wanted you right here with me, not because I want to be right and for you to be wrong. I wanted you right here with me so that you could understand that this is about so much more than what laws we pass as a nation. This is about whether or not we are right with God. You've picked and you've chosen. Why? You've picked and you've chosen because you know in your heart that there is sin and righteousness. You judged me at the beginning of this conversation because you believe that it's wrong for me to be judgmental. But, oh please understand something! You judged me for something you do, both in the sense that you pick and choose, just like I pick and choose. Secondly, you judged me for being judgmental, which means that you judged me for doing what you did.

You believe that there's a right and a wrong. What's your source? Here's what worries me. You believe there's a right and a wrong, and you believe your source is you. You believe you sit at the center of the universe. You believe that within you lies the capacity and the ability to determine in, of, and for yourself what is right and what is wrong. And I'm saying you don't even have the ability to wake yourself up in the morning. You do not have the ability to determine what's right and what's wrong. The heart is deceitful and wicked above all else; who can know it? You don't even know your own heart. You don't even know your own motivations.

You know what you need? You need one who is objectively righteous, who can point you to objective righteousness, so that you can strive for objective righteousness, recognize that you can't achieve objective righteousness, and then turn to the One who lived out objective righteousness in his active obedience to the Father, so that he would be objectively righteous and be able to impute righteousness to those of us who cannot live out objective righteousness, and then in his passive obedience took upon himself the penalty for those who were not objectively righteous, so that this double imputation could take place, that my sin imputed to him could be nailed to the cross and God could be just. And his righteousness could be imputed to me, so that God could justify the sinner and still be righteous and holy.

This is why this issue is so important. And this is why we can't compromise on this issue—because there is a right, there is a wrong, there is a God who will judge. And it is of no benefit to anyone for us to know that and not say that.

It is not kindness for me to watch my neighbor's house burn down and pray that he gets out. It is kindness to pick up the phone and call him while I'm running over to knock on his door, all the while prepared to kick it down if he doesn't answer, and drag him out if he can't walk out. That's loving my neighbor. Not watching my neighbor's house burn down and hoping that as he breathes his last he remembers—I was nice.

Let's pray. O gracious God, our Father, we bow before you as a humble and a grateful people. Humble because we recognize that we are indeed sinners in need of a Savior. Humble because we recognize that we are indeed hypocrites. Humble because we recognize that we are no better than anyone else who is at war with you and on the way to hell. Grateful because we recognize that in spite of our sinfulness, that in spite of our hypocrisy, that in spite of our unworthiness, Christ died for sin, once for all, the just for the unjust, in order that he might bring us back to God. Grateful because you made him who knew no sin to be sin for us that we might become the righteousness of God in him.

Grant by your grace that we might speak the truth to those who are perishing. Grant that we might know what we believe and why we believe it, and that we might be prepared to communicate it effectively and winsomely to those who would question us. Grant by your grace that we would be stewards of these great mysteries, that we would be proclaimers of these great truths, that we would preserve the pattern of sound words that we have been taught, that we would guard by the Holy Spirit that deposit that has been made in us, that we would study to show ourselves approved as workmen who don't need to be ashamed, because we handle accurately the Word of truth.

And in the midst of it all, we ask that you would be kind and merciful, not only with us, but with those around us. God, would you stay your hand of judgment? For we do know, realize, and believe, that if you don't judge America, you'll have to apologize to Sodom and Gomorrah. But might you be patient just a bit longer? Might you grant grace and mercy? Might you send the winds of revival? Might you remind us from whence we've come? Might you remind us of Whose we are? And might you remind us that there is a God—there is truth—there is right—there is wrong—there is guilt—there is grace—and there is salvation. Father, I pray for the one under the sound of my voice who has not come to you in repentance and faith through your Son Jesus Christ. Grant by your grace that they might hear and heed the truth of your Word, that they might flee to Christ and be found in him. This we pray in his name, pleading that Christ might have the fulness of the reward for which he died. And all God's people said, Amen.

Notes

Chapter One: What Is Expository Apologetics?

1. Loraine Boettner, *The Reformed Doctrine of Predestination*, Accordance electronic ed. (Grand Rapids, MI: Eerdmans, 1932), n.p.
2. Cornelius Van Til, *Christian Apologetics* (Phillipsburg, NJ: Presbyterian and Reformed, 1976), 1.
3. See Michael P. Farris, "Protecting Parental Rights: Why It Should Be a Priority," HSLDA website, Sept. 28, 2006.
4. Charter of New England, 1620.

Chapter Two: 1 Peter 3 and the Essence of Apologetics

1. The so-called "household code" passages give instructions to husbands, wives, children, and servants as to their proper role within the context of the family.
2. John Calvin, *Commentaries on the Catholic Epistles* in *Calvin's Commentaries* (Complete), trans. John King, Accordance electronic ed. (Edinburgh, UK: Calvin Translation Society, 1847), n.p.
3. J. P. Louw and Eugene Nida, eds., *Greek-English Lexicon of the New Testament: Based on Semantic Domains*, (New York: United Bible Societies, 1989), 1 Peter 3:9.
4. John Foxe, *Foxe's Book of Martyrs*, ed. William Byron Forbush, Accordance electronic ed. (Altamonte Springs, FL: OakTree Software, 1997), n.p.
5. Martin Luther, "A Mighty Fortress," 1529.
6. Simon J. Kistemaker, "James, Epistles of John, Peter and Jude," *New Testament Commentary* (Grand Rapids, MI: Baker, 1986), 134.
7. Ibid.
8. See Louw and Nida, *Greek-English Lexicon of the New Testament*, Galatians 1:10.

Chapter Three: Why Unbelief?

1. C. F. Keil and Franz Delitzsch, *Commentary on the Old Testament*, Accordance electronic ed. (Peabody, MA: Hendrickson, 1996), n.p.
2. Ibid.
3. John Murray, quoted in Douglas Moo, *The Epistle to the Romans*, The New International Commentary on the New Testament (Grand Rapids, MI: Eerdmans, 1996), 92.
4. Ibid.
5. Strong's *Greek Dictionary of the New Testament*, s.v. "moros," Accordance Bible Software.

6. Verlyn Verbrugge, ed., *The New International Theological Dictionary of New Testament Theology* (Grand Rapids, MI: Zondervan, 2000), s.v. "moros."
7. Ibid.
8. See G. K. Beale, *We Become What We Worship: A Biblical Theology of Idolatry* (Downers Grove, IL: InterVarsity Press, 2008). Note that Beale omits the word *like* in his title. He explains this in his introduction.
9. Thomas R. Schreiner, *Romans*, Baker Exegetical Commentary on the New Testament (Grand Rapids, MI: Baker Academic, 2008), 94.

Chapter Four: Paul's Expository Apologetic
1. See, for example, Paul's reference to Greek poets/philosophers in Acts 17.
2. Charles Hodge, *A Commentary on the Epistle to the Romans: Designed for Students of the English Bible* (Philadelphia: Grigg and Elliot, 1835), 400.

Chapter Five: Learning Apologetics through Confessions, Creeds, and Catechisms
1. James C. Robertson, *Sketches of Church History: From A.D. 33 to the Reformation*, Accordance electronic ed. (London: Society for Promoting Christian Knowledge, 1912), 46.
2. Voddie Baucham Jr., *The Ever-Loving Truth: Can Faith Thrive in a Post-Christian Culture?* (Nashville, TN: Broadman and Holman, 2008).
3. Charles Haddon Spurgeon, "Introduction to the Baptist Confession of Faith (1689)," http://www.spurgeon.org/~phil/creeds/bcof.htm.

Chapter Six: The Ten Commandments
1. Robert H. Mounce, *Matthew*, New International Biblical Commentary, Accordance electronic ed. (Peabody, MA: Hendrickson, 1991), 1:44.
2. Rosaria Butterfield, *The Secret Thoughts of an Unlikely Convert* (Pittsburgh, PA: Crown & Covenant, 2012), Kindle ed., locations 636–38.
3. Ibid.
4. John Calvin, *Commentary on Matthew, Mark, and Luke* in *Calvin's Commentaries* (Complete), trans. John King, Accordance electronic ed. (Edinburgh, UK: Calvin Translation Society, 1847), n.p.
5. John Frame's Christian Apologetics lectures are available through iTunes U, https://itunes.apple.com/us/course/christian-apologetics-dr./id537705979/.
6. Westminster Shorter Catechism.
7. George Washington's farewell address, 1796. Available through Yale Law School's Avalon project, avalon.law.yale.edu/18th_century/washing.asp.
8. Ibid.
9. Westminster Shorter Catechism.
10. Daniel Burke, "Update: Harvard's Satanic 'Black Mass' Cancelled," *CNN .com*, May 12, 2014, http://religion.blogs.cnn.com/2014/05/12/harvard-groups-plans-to-stage-black-mass-anger-catholics/.
11. Francis Scott Key, "The Star-Spangled Banner," 1814.
12. Westminster Shorter Catechism.
13. The Motion Picture Production Code of 1930 (Hays Code), ArtsReformation .com, http://www.artsreformation.com/a001/hays-code.html.
14. Ibid.
15. Westminster Shorter Catechism.

Chapter Seven: Basic Objections

1. Jerry Crowe, "Rainbow Man's Dark Side Keeps Him from Getting Out," *L. A. Times,* May 19, 2008, http://articles.latimes.com/2008/may/19/sports/sp -crowe19.
2. The term *clobber verse* is frequently used by homosexual advocates to describe the passages in the Bible that condemn homosexuality. The term is derogatory in that it infers a cherry-picking approach to the Bible as opposed to thoughtful exegesis, which, according to them, would actually lead to loving acceptance of homosexuality and same-sex marriage.
3. *The West Wing,* "The Midterms," season 2, episode 3.
4. Philip S. Ross, *From the Finger of God* (Ross-shire, UK: Christian Focus, 2010), 2.
5. Ibid.
6. Roya Nikkhah, "Grandmother and Grandson to Have Child Together," *The Telegraph,* July 21, 2014, http://www.telegraph.co.uk/news/newstopics/how aboutthat/7662232/Grandmother-and-grandson-to-have-child-together.html.
7. Jonathan Pearlman, "Australian Judge Says Incest May No Longer Be a Taboo," *The Telegraph,* July 17, 2014, http://www.telegraph.co.uk/news /worldnews/australiaandthepacific/australia/10958728/Australian-judge-says -incest-may-no-longer-be-a-taboo.html.
8. See Richard Barcellos, *An Ethical Manifesto: 1 Timothy 1:8–11 and the Deca- logue, Founders.org,* http://founders.org/fj36-2/an-ethical-manifesto-1-timothy -18-11-and-the-decalogue/.
9. Second London Baptist Confession, 19.3 (1689).
10. Robert Jamieson, A. R. Fausset, and David Brown, *Commentary Critical and Explanatory on the Whole Bible, 1871,* Accordance electronic ed. (Altamonte Springs, FL: OakTree Software, 1996), n.p.
11. Ross, *From the Finger of God,* 16.

Chapter Eight: The Expository Apologetic Waltz

1. Roger R. Nicole, "Polemic Theology: How to Deal with Those Who Differ from Us," Founders.org, http://Founders.org/.
2. See, for example, "Active Listening: Hear What People Are Really Saying," *MindTools,* http://www.mindtools.com/CommSkll/ActiveListening.htm.
3. Mortimer J. Adler, *How to Speak, How to Listen* (New York: Touchstone, 1997), Kindle ed.
4. Ibid.
5. Ibid.

Chapter Nine: Preaching and Teaching Like an Expository Apologist

1. The word, *epagōnizesthai,* translated *contend* in the ESV, literally means to struggle for; to agonize greatly; to exert intense effort on behalf of something. See J. P. Louw and Eugene Nida, eds., *Greek-English Lexicon of the New Testament: Based on Semantic Domains,* (New York: United Bible Societies, 1989), Jude 3.
2. James C. Robertson, *Sketches of Church History: From A.D. 33 to the Refor- mation,* Accordance electronic ed. (London: Society for Promoting Christian Knowledge, 1912), 43.

General Index

abomination, 127, 128, 182–83
abortion, 122, 135, 186
academy, objections in, 173–74
active listening, 149
Acts
    expository apologetics in, 76–82
    evangelism in, 169
Adam, 79
Adler, Mortimer J., 148–49
adultery, 107, 109
"all truth is God's truth," 153
ambassadors for Christ, 170
America, biblical and theological foundations of, 114–17
"answer a fool" strategy, 49, 72–73
answering honest questions, 64
answering objections, 21
antinomianism, 71
apologetics
    for everybody, 26–27, 35, 38
    as formal debate, 20–21
    with Gentile audience, 76
    with Jewish audience, 76–77
    as merely answering questions, 62
    as philosophical, 34–35
    training in, 87
Apostles' Creed, 88–89
apostleship, 74
application, as essence of discipleship, 179
arguing with yourself, 163–64
Arianism, 90
Arminius, 176
arrogance, 143

"assembly line" approach to discipleship, 178–79
Athanasian Creed, 92–95
atheism, 58–59, 125
attitude, of apologist, 38–39
audiences, of expository apologetics, 26–31
Augsburg Confession (1530), 95
Augustine, 176

Baptist Catechism (1813), 136
Barth, Karl, 148
basics, of expository apologetics, 34
Beale, G. K., 54
Begg, Alistair, 111
Belgic Confession of Faith (1561), 96
Benjamin Keach's Catechism (1693), 136
bestiality, 129
Bible
    and apologetics, 20, 34
    authority of, 20, 130
    contains basics of apologetics, 34
biblical illiteracy, 24–25
biblical objections, 176–77
Bin Laden, Osama, 60
Black, Jack, 128–29
"black Mass" (at Harvard), 118–19
blessing, in face of insult, 39
blindness, 53
Boettner, Loraine, 19–20
boldness, 151
Borg, Marcus, 174
Bruggencate, Sye Ten, 65
Butterfield, Rosaria, 109

Scripture Index

Also Available from Voddie Baucham Jr.

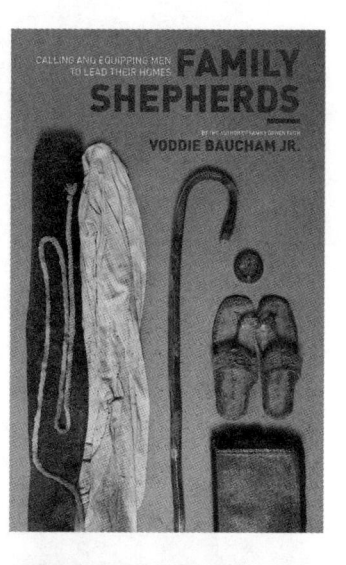